American Trade Policy

American Trade Policy

A Tragedy in the Making

Anne O. Krueger

THE AEI PRESS

Publisher for the American Enterprise Institute
WASHINGTON, D.C.

1995

The American Enterprise Institute would like to thank the Sasakawa Peace Foundation and the American Express Foundation for their support of this project.

Distributed to the Trade by National Book Network, 15200 NBN Way, Blue Ridg Summit, PA 17214. To order call toll free 1-800-462-6420 or 1-717-794-380(For all other inquiries please contact the AEI Press, 1150 Seventeenth Street, N.W Washington, D.C. 20036 or call 1-800-862-5801.

Library of Congress Cataloging-in-Publication Data

Krueger, Anne O.
    American trade policy : a tragedy in the making / Anne O. Krueger.
      p. cm.
    Includes bibliographical references and index.
    ISBN 0-8447-3888-3. — ISBN 0-8447-3889-1 (pbk.)
    1. United States—Commercial policy. 2. United States—Foreign economic relations. I. Title.
    HF1455.K83 1995
    382'.3'0973—dc20   95-9946
                                          CIP

ISBN 0-8447-3888-3 (alk. paper)
ISBN 0-8447-3889-1 (pbk.: alk. paper)

THE AEI PRESS
Publisher for the American Enterprise Institute
1150 17th Street, N.W., Washington, D.C. 20036

Contents

Acknowledgments

Whenever policy issues are analyzed, a difficulty arises in that the issues themselves may be a moving target. It is unlikely that the problem was ever any greater than it was in the course of developing this monograph: the fortunes of the North American Free Trade Agreement and the Uruguay Round seemed constantly to change.

In a changing policy environment, the comments, suggestions, and support of colleagues are even more valuable than is normally the case. My deepest debt is to Claude Barfield, who provided moral support and many suggestions in the course of this project. I am also indebted to Steve Charnowitz, Mac Destler, Michael Finger, Isaiah Frank, Jules Katz, Patrick Low, and Pietro Nivola for valuable comments and suggestions on the penultimate draft of this monograph. Roderick Duncan provided not only valuable research assistance, but useful comments and suggestions throughout the course of the work. Finally, I am indebted to the American Enterprise Institute for financial support for the project.

Anne O. Krueger

1

The Devil Is in the Details

The increasing integration of the world economy has been a hallmark of economic advancement over the past two centuries. As costs of transport and communications have fallen, economic interactions between distant people, which were earlier limited to occasional shipments of exotic low-volume, high-value luxury goods such as silk and spices, extended first to trade in vital and reasonably durable bulk commodities such as foodgrains, and then—in the past several decades—to daily air shipments of specialized parts and components, high-tech items, and even repairmen, other specialists, and fresh-cut flowers.

As that has happened, the importance of the open multilateral trading system as a linchpin of high and rising productivity and living standards has increased. But so, too, has the visibility of foreign competition, as the insulation earlier provided by high transport costs and long intervals of time for shipment and communications has greatly diminished.

Ironically, when trade was less important, leadership of the open multilateral system was left largely in the hands of statesmen and mandarins whose primary concern was the system as a whole. In the nineteenth century, Britain led the world in establishing and underpinning the international economic system, with virtually free trade and London as a financial center. When British hegemony diminished and the system broke down in the period before World War II, it was American leadership that restored the open multilateral trading system and led the world toward trade liberalization in the postwar period.

In the early postwar years American trade was an extremely small percentage of gross national product: in some years exports did not even reach 5 percent of GNP, and imports were smaller still. The Department of State spearheaded American leadership of the open trading system: trade policy was seen largely as a matter of foreign policy and the national interest.[1] As worldwide trade was liberalized and Europe and Japan recovered from the war, the importance of trade to the American economy increased (although trade as a percentage of GNP is still small in contrast to most other major trading nations). Simultaneously, trade policy came increasingly to be formulated by those more susceptible to pressures of special interest groups and less well positioned to defend the "public interest" than in the immediate postwar years.[2] That shift is ironic because the trade policy adopted as foreign policy was in fact more conducive to the economic health of the American economy than is trade policy carried out in response to protectionist pressures. The shift toward trade policy in response to special interests has come at a time when the importance of an open trade policy and of an open international trading system has never been greater.

Part of the reason why special interest groups are able to exert unusual influence over trade policy lies in the fact that it is inherently complex.[3] The North American Free Trade Agreement is 2,000 pages long; procedures governing antidumping and countervailing duty complaints are understood by few other than lawyers specializing in them. Despite a several-hundred-page compendium assembled every other year by the House Ways and Means Committee of the *important* U.S. trade laws, no one can possibly master them all.

Moreover, the effects of trade policies are rarely intuitively evident. The consumer buying sugar in a supermarket does not recog-

---

1. See Baldwin (1985) for an exposition. The U.S. economy was at that time very large relative to the rest of the world, and world prices were, in effect, U.S. dollar prices. That fact may have facilitated the acceptance of trade policy as foreign policy in the early postwar years.

2. The shift is by no means complete, as evidenced by the congressional approval of the North American Free Trade Agreement and the completion of the Uruguay Round of GATT negotiations. Nonetheless, the exceptions necessary to achieve either of those results were considerably greater than they would have been in earlier years.

3. Those seeking advantages from trade policy also work to find ways to make it difficult for the public to ascertain the extent to which they are benefiting. They also use arguments that they believe will be most effective, even when those arguments have little relevance to the real reasons for seeking protection. For interesting examples, see Bovard (1991a).

nize that the sugar price is more than twice the world price; even bakers and candy makers for years failed to oppose U.S. sugar policy.[4] Arguments that foreign cars "cost Americans jobs" ignore three facts. First, most jobs associated with automobiles are in industries servicing them, including road construction and maintenance, filling stations, repair services, and dealerships. Lower car prices mean more cars owned by Americans, which in turn result in more jobs in auto-related industries, even if the cars are imported. Second, when we buy some commodities from foreigners, they buy others from us.[5] Third, monetary, fiscal, and exchange rate policies all have a lot more to do with the level of employment than do imports of particular commodities. Few purchasers of cars in the 1980s recognized that they were paying approximately $2,000 more for their (domestic and imported) cars because of a voluntary export restraint agreement negotiated with Japan.

If citizens could easily identify and directly vote on the magnitudes of gains and losses and the identities of the winners and losers from trade restrictions, there is little doubt that American trade policy would be different. Who can believe that American voters would accept an average payment of over $500,000 per sugar farm, when there are fewer than 135,000 workers—many of them immigrants permitted to enter the United States to work in the cane fields—employed in cane production on 12,500 farms? If the damage to the Florida Everglades from the expansion of land use for water-intensive sugar (which is profitable only because of the sugar program) were known, opposition would intensify still further. Yet, in fact, the U.S. sugar program remains among the most sacrosanct of U.S. protectionist programs (Krueger 1990). Would voters approve protection to domestic automobile producers—adding the $2,000 per car already noted and conservatively estimated to cost $105,000 per year per job saved[6]—that did little (and may even have been counterproductive) to improve the competitive position of U.S. automobile producers?

---

4. Sugar growers long opposed proposed changes in the means of protecting sugar to "deficiency payments" rather than price supports. The apparent reason was the belief that, if the public were aware of the size of the deficiency payments made to individual growers (equivalent to what they receive through price supports), there would be strong opposition to continuation of those payments (Krueger 1990).

5. See chapter 2, where I address the fallacious idea that the commodity composition of trade affects our balance of payments.

6. The estimate is from Hufbauer, Berliner, and Elliott (1986, 258) and pertains to the year 1984. Alternative estimates they cited are more than 50 percent higher than this.

But the fact that the gainers and losers, and the magnitudes of the spoils, are unknown is no accident. The lack of visibility of results, combined with the complexity of trade regulations, is the way trade policy is now done. It has given special interests seeking protection greater and greater influence over the particulars of trade policy affecting them. They have been able to advocate obscure provisions of trade laws, influence free trade agreements, and lobby for other regulations to help their particular industries, with little or no visible opposition. Almost always, measures that patently will give those advocating them an artificial competitive edge over their rivals are defended as "preserving the environment," "protecting the health and safety of American consumers," or "ensuring fair trade." In fact, other measures could achieve comparable results with far lower costs to American consumers (and far less advantage to the producers advocating the more costly measures). Indeed, in extreme cases the only significant effect of the more costly measures is to increase profits for those in the industry.

Because many provisions of trade law and trade practice are not readily understood by anyone other than those in the industry, the public has voiced much less opposition to protectionist measures than would have arisen had the true effects and costs of those measures been widely known and understood.

Special interests have been able to achieve that result by hiding their self-interest in intervention behind appeals to the public that America's trading partners engage in "unfair" trading practices. Those complaints have mounted in ferocity in recent years and have influenced trading relations with virtually all America's trading partners. Japan, however, has borne the brunt of the bashing. Headlines in American newspapers tell how U.S. trade negotiators are going to Japan to "force" the Japanese to change certain practices, with little attention to whether U.S. firms engage in similar practices, whether the United States would be responsive to similar efforts to "force" American trade policy into a certain mold, or even whether the Japanese or others actually engage in the "unfair" practices of concern. Things have progressed so far that we now demand that the Japanese guarantee quantitative results that governments cannot achieve except through the very types of intervention we say we object to their doing! (See chapter 4.) The United States has even had the effrontery to assert that closed Japanese markets for rice (which definitely harm the Japanese and natural rice exporters such as Thailand) harm American farmers,[7] despite the fact that the various subsidies and protec-

---

7. "U.S. Rice Farmers Pressing Again for Entry into the Japanese Market," *New York Times*, March 25, 1989, p. 17.

tion given to U.S. rice growers are estimated to have a producer subsidy equivalent of over 50 percent in every year between 1985 and 1988 (GATT 1989, 237). It would not be profitable to export American rice at world prices without domestic subsidies, yet that goes unnoticed in trade discussions.

The public's political support of, or at least acquiescence to, protection has recently been bolstered by concerns about American competitiveness, the current account balance, and employment opportunities. Although economists have long since pointed out that the current account balance and the level of employment are macroeconomic phenomena little affected by trade policies and practices either abroad or at home, those seeking protection have veiled their arguments in appeals for support of the unemployed and the need for greater competitiveness. Those arguments, although largely fallacious, have made it easier for politicians to approve the policies special interest groups advocate.

The tension between American systemic interests in the open multilateral system and the special interests influencing trade policy reached crisis proportions in the debate over NAFTA. While in the end the "public interest" won, as I shall discuss below, it did not do so without concessions to special interests, and, worse yet, the arguments opponents put forth were incredibly protectionist and alarmist. Given that American tariffs against goods imported from Mexico averaged around 4 percent, that Mexican imports into the United States constituted around 5 percent of total imports, and that the relative productivity of American workers compared with Mexican workers exceeded the wage differential, it was hard to believe that serious people could possibly think that such great damage could come from such a small reduction in tariffs and trade barriers (to be phased in over a ten- to fifteen-year period).

The NAFTA debate, if it did nothing else, proved that the importance of the open multilateral system for the United States is either taken for granted with far too much complacency or not understood at all.[8] And, despite the fact that NAFTA passed and that the Uruguay Round came to a generally successful conclusion, it was evident in

---

8. As I shall discuss below, an individual genuinely believing in an open multilateral trading system might legitimately have objected to NAFTA on the grounds that preferential regional arrangements were a departure from the nondiscrimination that a multilateral system implies. As the debate evolved, however, it became important for the GATT round that NAFTA pass. In addition, raising those questions would have provided support for protectionist interests.

both forums that special interests play an increasingly important role in American trade policy to the detriment of the national interest.[9]

There are two, interrelated challenges to American support of the open multilateral system. The first is the increasing importance of producer groups in influencing trade policy. The second is the inevitable distractions that NAFTA will provide for policy makers. Any preferential trading arrangement is inherently discriminatory among trading partners: under some circumstances, such an arrangement can be consistent with an open multilateral trading system. Whether NAFTA (and its possible extension to other Western Hemisphere countries) will or will not be consistent depends on the degree of support the multilateral trading system receives in the aftermath of the Uruguay Round, especially from the United States. Support will entail both the active participation in founding the new World Trade Organization *and* eschewing practices, especially bilateral arrangements, that are not consistent with our obligations under the GATT or the WTO. Whether American officials concerned with trade policy—surrounded as they are by producer protectionist pressures and regional interests—can devote sufficient time, attention, and commitment to the open multilateral system is an important question.

The purpose of this monograph is to argue that American trade policy has become increasingly schizophrenic as fear of competition and pressures from special interests influence a variety of sectoral policies even as we continue to assert our support for an open multilateral system. That schizophrenia in turn is leading to a number of dangers that confront the international trading system as a whole. The United States is far too important a trading nation for the system to flourish in the absence of strong American support.

In the years immediately after World War II, the United States provided leadership in developing an open multilateral trading system, under which trading nations agreed to adhere to a common set of policies. Those policies included a most-favored-nation clause[10] in

---

9. See, for example, Orden (forthcoming) for a description of the arrangements made with respect to various agricultural interests in return for their support of NAFTA.

10. Various trading nations intermittently used the most-favored-nation clause throughout the nineteenth and early twentieth centuries. The clause came to be a central feature of American trade policy in the 1930s under Secretary of State Cordell Hull. See Dam (1970) for a brief account. The Reciprocal Trade Agreements Act of 1934 authorized bilateral negotiations for reductions of trade barriers (hence the name reciprocal), in return for which the parties signed treaties that accorded the partner MFN status. U.S. policy had shifted to an MFN clause after 1923. See Haberler (1933, 362ff.) for a brief history.

bilateral trading treaties, which implied that each country would receive treatment "no less favorable" than the most favored nation.[11] In addition, nations eschewed the use of nontariff barriers to trade except in exceptional circumstances and participated in multilateral trade negotiations to reduce tariff barriers throughout the world.

The most-favored-nation clause meant that each member country would be treated alike. Placing sole reliance upon tariffs ensured some transparency in trade policy: those interested could find out the amount of protection received by import-competing producers by consulting a tariff schedule. Participating in multilateral trade negotiations provided an effective mechanism under which exporters in each country would provide political support for tariff reductions and trade liberalization, thus offsetting the pressures of import-competing interests for protection.

Under the GATT, trade was greatly liberalized, and the world economy grew at unprecedented rates in the quarter century after the war. From the late 1950s until at least the early 1980s, observers could readily conclude that trade between nations had never been so free as it had become, and that the long-term trend, at least among the industrialized countries, had been for continuing trade liberalization. While real world GNP had grown at rates never before realized over such a long period of time, the growth of world trade had proceeded almost twice as rapidly.

By any standard, therefore, the open multilateral trading system served the world well. In recent years, however, political pressures against the system have mounted. The United States has, for a variety of reasons, failed to exercise leadership in support of the open multilateral system. Loss of that support has been critical for the system as a whole.

Over the years, American trade policy has gradually drifted toward an approach to trading relations in which there are strong bilateral elements. That drift has not been the outcome of any conscious shift in policy, but rather the result of a slow erosion of the commitment to multilateralism, and the ability of those seeking protection to cloak their pressures under the guise of seeking "fair trade," which then results in country-by-country, bilateral negotiations.[12] The drift still continues.

---

11. The GATT permits customs unions and free trade areas. But for them to be GATT-consistent, they must be across-the-board and not sectoral arrangements, they must not raise tariffs or other trade barriers against third countries, and they must cover "substantially all trade" or be interim arrangements toward that end.

12. See Nivola (1993) for an effort to explain this drift. Nivola concludes that there is no set of compelling reasons for the shift.

Trade policy is vitally important not only to the future health of the American and world economies, but also to international political relations. I shall argue that the drift to bilateralism inevitably increases the protection given to American producers and that the attempts to achieve protection from foreign competition in fact distract American firms from increasing their own efficiency and competitiveness. It is simply more attractive to produce in a market sheltered from competition than to expend the effort to reduce costs and to increase efficiency. Moreover, the present bilateral approach to trade policy is gradually undermining the open multilateral trading system that has been serving the entire global economy so well—at a time when the need is to strengthen the system. Should that system gradually weaken, the entire globe will lose, and American productivity and living standards will suffer along with those of other countries. One can even argue that the capture of trade policy by special interests may prospectively damage the democratic process, as citizens discover the true driving forces behind it.

This monograph explains the tragedy of current U.S. trade policy. The next chapter provides background for the analysis. First, I examine the economists' traditional case for free trade. Then I recount the role of the United States in the evolution of the open multilateral trading system from World War II to the 1970s.

Thereafter, the next several chapters review the main aspects of American trade policy. Chapter 3 discusses the drift away from multilateralism. Chapter 4 discusses the increasing U.S. tendency to rely on "administered protection," which has a strong element of protectionism and bilateralism in it. Chapter 5 covers regional trading arrangements. Chapter 6 then summarizes the arguments and pleads for a renewed commitment to, and leadership in support of, the multilateral trading system.

2

American Leadership and the Open Multilateral Trading System under the GATT

Ever since Adam Smith first elucidated the ways in which decisions made by individuals in a market setting can serve the social good "as if by an invisible hand," the case for free trade has been clear: it makes no sense to produce goods at home if other items can be produced more cheaply and exchanged for them. A nation's productive resources are limited. When consumers demand greater quantities of one commodity, the nation must attract resources from other economic activities to increase domestic output of the good. When that good is relatively cheaper from a foreign source, trade provides an "alternative technology" to domestic production: it requires the diversion of fewer resources to produce goods with which to finance the importation of the commodity than it does to produce the commodity domestically. Living standards can thus be higher.

The Case for Free Trade

The argument for free trade based on comparative advantage and the division of labor is simply an extension of the common-sense allocation of resources by individuals within an economy. A lawyer hires a secretary because his time is more valuable when spent practicing law; he can earn more by paying the secretary and using his time to serve more clients. In a like vein, countries' citizens will be better off

TABLE 2-1
WORLD TRADE AND TRADE IN MANUFACTURES, 1950 TO 1990

Year	Exports (billions of U.S. dollars)		Percent of World Exports	
	World	Manufactures	From U.S.	Of Manufactures
1950	61	23	16.7	37.7
1960	129	64	17.9	49.7
1970	312	190	14.7	60.9
1980	1,989	1,097	11.8	55.1
1990	3,485	2,445	11.9	70.2

SOURCE: GATT, *International Trade*, various issues. Geneva.

using their time and other resources to produce those items for which the return is highest.

Recently, economists have begun to focus as well on "intraindustry" trade. That is trade that takes place within an industrial category, as firms manufacture different products to satisfy a wide variety of particular demands and specialized uses that characterize modern industrial society. Usually, production of each variety requires a firm to incur certain fixed costs. The more the firm produces, the lower its average cost of production.

In those circumstances markets are "imperfectly competitive," and entrepreneurs produce new varieties as long as they can reasonably expect to cover their average costs (including fixed costs) of production. A larger market permits lower average costs of production and a wider variety of goods. Under imperfect competition traders enjoy both the "comparative advantage" benefits that arise because of different cost structures and the "variety" and "length of production run" benefits that accrue because trade permits a larger scale of production of a wider variety of goods.[1]

Intraindustry trade takes place both in consumer goods and in goods used in production. Everyone is familiar with the variety of automobiles, appliances, and many other consumer goods. In the case of producer goods, availability of a wide variety of specialized

---

1. The increased importance of intraindustry trade can be seen in part from the numbers in table 2-1. As the last column makes clear, the percentage of manufactures in total exports rose sharply over the postwar period. The trend toward a greater proportional concentration of trade in manufactures has been continuous since World War II, except during the 1970s, when the fourfold increase in the price of oil resulted in a much higher share of oil in world trade and thus reduced the share of everything else.

parts, machines, and materials is essential for modern production techniques. Unfettered access to the international economy is essential if producers are to be internationally competitive: if they must pay more for certain inputs than their foreign competitors, they are at a serious disadvantage when competing in international markets.

In addition to enabling domestic consumers and producers to obtain goods more cheaply and to sell in a wider market, free trade increases the degree of competition within a domestic economy.[2] Just as Smith pointed to the invisible hand, he also recognized that monopolies would tend to harm social welfare. Free trade reduces the monopoly power of individual producers; protection inevitably increases it.

Recently, economists have also been investigating the role of trade in providing ready access to improvements in technology. The international transmission of knowledge is clearly important: once new knowledge has been created in any part of the world, there is no point in allocating resources in other countries to create it all over again. Trade in goods and services speeds the transmission of knowledge and hence can lead to higher growth not only in individual countries, but also in the world as a whole.

Arguments against Protection. The positive arguments for free trade are probably convincing in themselves. Experience with protection, however, has provided a number of additional reasons why an open economy best suits countries desirous of maintaining or improving their international competitiveness and raising their living standards.

As the structure of industry has become more complex, the arguments for relying on markets and opposing protection have, if anything, become stronger. As the variety of goods and services produced has reached the billions (if not trillions), the amount of specialized knowledge and capacity required for production has made it more infeasible than ever for government decision makers to have the necessary information to allocate resources and to identify the economic activities to be favored. When there were few manufacturing activities, and production was fairly standardized in a narrow range of goods, the information with which to make decisions was

---

2. That is especially important when there are significant fixed costs: if domestic industries with high fixed costs enjoy protection, it may not pay for anyone else to enter the market, so that those already producing the goods will have sizable monopoly power.

relatively accessible to government officials.[3] As such specialized knowledge as the tensile strength of alternative materials, the properties of different chemicals, or the engineering characteristics of alternative designs has become increasingly important in business decisions, the feasibility of informed decision making, or even careful monitoring, by government officials has declined sharply. For the same reasons, the susceptibility of the public and of politicians to special influence pleading has increased. Recently, the collapse of most of the centrally planned economies has dramatically demonstrated the consequences of bureaucratic decisions on resource allocation. Central planning offices could not monitor the behavior of managers; only decentralized incentives could spur appropriate decisions.

The problems inherent in bureaucratic decision making in general apply with equal force to bureaucratic or political decisions regarding which industries "deserve" protection. Those with political influence choose the arguments they believe will be most persuasive to policy makers in seeking protection. Policy makers cannot possibly have the information on which to base informed decisions.[4] In consequence, protection more often than not is accorded to the politically more powerful, and such economic criteria as might make sense have little influence.[5]

Another major defect of protection is that it inevitably discriminates against export industries and others not receiving protection. Since those industries normally are the most competitive industries, protection in effect provides more resources to the relatively less productive sectors of the economy at the expense of the more productive. By definition, the authorities cannot protect everyone:[6] when the rela-

---

3. That is probably the reason that the economic costs of government regulations and controls in developing countries became so evident in the 1980s: many of those countries had started with very large agricultural sectors and very small manufacturing bases. As they had pursued their development strategies, however, success inevitably resulted in the increasing diversification of production. As that happened, information on which to base resource allocation decisions became more specialized and therefore more inaccessible to economic planners.

4. Note that decisions about protection must be based on judgments about the future—something inherently uncertain and risky. From the viewpoint of those who do receive protection from foreign competition, uncertainty is automatically reduced.

5. In practice, there is considerable evidence that nations confer protection when few industry groups oppose it.

6. To be sure, one could have tariffs on all imports and a subsidy in similar

tive prices of import-competing goods rise, the relative prices of other goods fall. Resources are then naturally pulled toward the import-competing industries, and exports shrink. Discrimination against the more productive and competitive activities increases when other producers pay more than the international price for their inputs, as they do when their suppliers are protected from foreign competition.

There is yet another related, but separate, consideration. Incentives for efficient production diminish if managers, when confronted with competitive pressures, believe that they can survive by seeking protection.[7] The very fact that they have a chance to escape the negative consequences of competition may induce them to react less strongly than they otherwise would when confronted with increasing competition from abroad. In addition, however, if managers' attentions are diverted from finding lower cost ways to deliver higher quality goods to lobbying for protection in Washington, reduced attention to improving competitiveness must inevitably result.

Finally, but perhaps most important, individual businesses necessarily assess uncertain future prospects when they make their decisions, and they must base those decisions on highly specific engineering and other plans. If managers know that they will be protected when decisions are erroneous, the likelihood that decision making will promote efficient competitive American industries is greatly reduced.

Exceptions to the Arguments for Free Trade. To be sure, one can in theory find exceptions to the arguments for free trade, although the conditions under which the theoretical cases for protection are valid are highly restrictive. One argument often used in developing countries is that there may be infant industries, already developed elsewhere, that could develop comparative advantage if they were protected for an initial period. Such an argument implies that there must be "spillover" effects, as otherwise individual investors would find it worth their while to accept initial losses in anticipation of future returns. It also implies that protection must be temporary. Despite its theoretical validity, the infant industry argument has been applied in many developing countries with dismal results. In any

---

proportion on exports. But for trade purposes, the result would be the same as a change in the exchange rate.

7. See Scherer (1992, 188) for a fascinating account of firm reactions to competition when seeking protection is one of the choices: "[I]n both the short run and the long run, companies' R&D spending responded less aggressively on average to import shocks of given magnitude when trade barriers were in place."

event, the infant industry argument can have little relevance for an advanced industrial economy, such as the United States.

A second argument has to do with national defense. Policy makers have argued that there may be some economic activities that are inherently high-cost domestically, but that should nonetheless have their capacity maintained, so that there would be no supply disruption in the event of war. There may be such industries. Even if there are, however, three conditions must be satisfied. First, the commodity must be cheaper to store than to produce in peacetime. Second, there must be supply locations unlikely to be affected by any hostilities (Canada and Mexico, for example, in the case of the United States). Third, there must be a genuine defense rationale.[8]

When proponents apply the national defense argument for protection to high-tech industries, they often couch it in terms of the necessity for America's defense establishment to have access to the latest and best high technology. That raises an interesting question: if protection is necessary, is it not because American firms are not competing effectively at the technological frontier? Are defense interests served by raising trade barriers, which is tantamount to recognizing that American producers will continue to lag behind?[9] Is not the argument equally compelling that the pressures of competition should be maintained precisely for national defense reasons?

Recently, a third type of argument has been propounded: there may be industries which by their nature are oligopolistic and in which first entrants will get the oligopoly or monopoly rents or profits. In fact, critical scrutiny of some of the cases in which proponents of intervention have suggested that those circumstances exist (supersonic aircraft and HDTV,[10] for example) indicates that they have often been wrong.[11] "Picking the winners" is more easily said than done!

---

8. All sorts of industries, including watch, scissor, and clothing manufacturers, have appealed for protection on national defense grounds. Perhaps the most ludicrous case of protection purportedly motivated by national defense concerns was in the period before 1960, when the United States had oil—a nonrenewable resource—import quotas for which the stated purpose was to maintain domestic productive capacity in the event of war! See Dam (1971) for an account.

9. Recall Scherer's finding that protection on average makes firms less aggressive in competing.

10. See Beltz (1991) for an account of the failure of Japanese intervention in HDTV contrasted with the evident American success in the absence of support for a "winner." See Baldwin and Krugman (1988) for an analysis of the aircraft industry.

11. See also Richardson (1989) for a survey of all empirical findings to that time with respect to the possible applicability of the argument.

There are, however, even stronger arguments against discriminatory case-by-case protection than that. They center on two related propositions. First, once protection is seen as a legitimate instrument of economic policy, all sorts of groups will pressure for protection. The political process is ineffective against strong interest groups, and the likelihood of receiving protection will be related more to political strength than to the degree to which the situation conforms to a theoretical exception to the free trade case. Second, even if the first argument could somehow be overcome, and a single country could improve its position through selective "scientific" intervention according to the precepts of efficient dynamic resource allocation, all would be worse off in a world in which many countries were attempting to implement interventionist trade policies.

Any examination of the structure of U.S. protection[12] provides strong evidence of the first proposition and of the importance of political strength, contrasted with economic merit, in determining protection levels.[13] There are relatively high levels of protection for some apparently declining industries (textiles and clothing), dynamic industries (semiconductors), defense industries (maritime shipping and machine tools), Rust Belt industries (steel and automobiles), and a number of agricultural products including peanuts, fruits and vegetables, cotton, tobacco, some dairy products, merino sheep, and sugar. For most of those industries, the estimated cost of protection per job saved is very high, while the benefits are arguably quite small. When we consider the pattern of protection as a whole, it makes even less sense.

The second proposition, while evident in theory, is less easy to prove, but probably of particular importance for the United States, given its role as the world's largest trading nation and its historical leadership role in the international economy. Any nation adopting protection against the imports from another invites a protective response, although the GATT rules provide a framework for avoiding some retaliation. In the case of the United States, however, policies that weaken the international trading system are almost bound to boomerang against American exporters. For one thing, the United States is sufficiently large that when we do take measures to reduce imports from our trading partners, our partners are usually con-

---

12. See Hufbauer, Berliner, and Elliott (1986) and Hufbauer and Elliott (1994) for an analysis of the existing structure of U.S. protection. See also the GATT (1989, 1994) reports and Krueger (1993c).

13. Even the advocates of intervention, such as Tyson (1992, 11), recognize that existing policies are chaotic and "counterproductive."

15

strained either to increase their exports to third markets (often then competing with us) or to reduce their imports from the rest of the world, including the United States.

The current schizophrenic policies give rise to an even more frightening possibility, however: our actions, even if they are designed in ways that American officials believe are "fair," may induce countermeasures by foreign governments. Those measures, in turn, may prompt yet further reactions from the United States. While the magnitudes of losses that would be incurred should a full-fledged "trade war" break out are so enormous that no responsible government would willingly risk them, American policies nonetheless run the risk of retaliation, which in turn could trigger a chain of events leading to a devastating trade war. To date, countries have mutually understood the catastrophe that would result from a breakdown of the world trading system. For that reason, nations have thus far resolved trade disputes rather than risk the consequences of an all-out trade war. Given the extent to which interdependence among countries has increased, the importance of international sourcing, and the extent to which many companies are purchasing and selling in a global market, the dislocation attendant upon an all-out trade war is virtually unthinkable.

While a risk of disaster does not prove certainty, the increasing American aggressiveness in international trading relations runs that risk. It is difficult to imagine the various nations of the world, and especially the large trading nations, each pursuing independent and unilateral policies to protect and support their own industries *without* major trade disputes arising. While each dispute may have a reasonably high probability of resolution because of fear of a trade war, only one failure will break down the system. Should the United States resort to "retaliation" against Japan, and Japan decide to pursue countermeasures by imposing barriers against imports from the United States, it might only be a small step before the European Community decided that it, too, would protect against Japanese imports. Once having done that, it might not be a far cry for Americans to protect against European competition, and for Europeans in turn to retaliate against American competition. The breakdown of the trading world into regional trading blocs could result.

The situation is even more worrisome because most Americans, including evidently American policy makers, appear to believe that the American economy is open and that only other countries are guilty of protection. The contrast between American words and American actions makes the risk of trade war even more likely than it would otherwise be. The purpose of the next several chapters is to

16

convince the reader that American economic policies have been considerably more protectionist and unilateral than American perceptions of those policies.

To avoid the breakdown of the world trading system, all major trading nations must join the international economic system and comply with its rules. As I shall discuss next, that system has served the world well, but it is now under threat. While a sudden, dramatic collapse has little likelihood, there is a strong possibility of gradual erosion and, ultimately, over one item or another, the outbreak of a trade war in which both sides stand firm, impose retaliatory tariffs, and engage in a cycle of counterretaliation. Neither side would anticipate the outcome. Each would expect the other to retreat, and with such tragic miscalculations, the unthinkable could happen. Indeed, perhaps the biggest single argument against current U.S. trade policy is that it greatly increases the risks of such a miserable outcome.

Fallacious Arguments for Protection. To this point, each of the arguments providing for an exception to the free trade precept has a theoretical justification, even if there are strong practical reasons for believing that those justifications have extremely limited, if any, applicability. Those seeking protection frequently put forward two other arguments, both of which economists unanimously believe are fallacious and without any justification—theoretical or empirical. The first is the mistaken belief that protection may reduce the American current account deficit. The second is the erroneous belief that protection can significantly affect the level of employment in the aggregate.[14]

The magnitude of the account deficit or surplus is determined by a country's savings-investment ratio. By definition, a country's current account balance equals its excess of saving over investment: when saving exceeds investment, the current account is positive, and domestic residents are acquiring foreign assets. To see this, recognize that the only way a society can spend more than it earns is by purchasing from others while financing those purchases with the sale of assets.[15] The mirror image to a current account deficit (surplus) is a capital account surplus (deficit). Surplus on the capital account is nothing other than the net sale of assets to foreigners.

---

14. In countries with a very high minimum wage, it is possible that protection may permit expansion of employment in the short run. If new wage bargains or higher minimum wages follow protection, however, the effect will be at best transitory, or additional protection would be needed.

15. The "sale of assets" includes borrowing from abroad. When a domestic resident borrows from a foreigner, he is "selling" an asset (his IOU) to the foreigner in exchange for purchasing power.

A little reflection indicates why protection cannot significantly affect the overall figures. First, the determinants of saving and investment are largely domestic in nature; they are little influenced by the factors determining protection. Suppose, for example, that a country increases protection to a particular industry. The domestic price of the item in question increases. That, in turn, induces consumers to shift part of their expenditures to other commodities (which implies either more imports of those commodities or fewer exports of the commodities consumers are now purchasing).[16] To provide increased supplies of the other goods and services demanded, either domestic production must increase (diverting production away from exportable or import-competing production and therefore resulting in an offsetting change in the trade balance) or imports must increase to satisfy demand. Either way, those mechanisms largely offset any reduction in imports of the protected commodity.

In addition, foreign producers of the import experience a reduced demand for their commodity because of protection. As a result, they shift their resources to other uses and either increase exports of other commodities or increase their production of commodities that compete with their imports—that include "our" exports. Either way, the current account balance tends even more to return to its initial levels. In fact, unless protection affects income distribution so as to change the general level of saving and investment, any remaining change in the current account balance will likely lead to an adjustment in the exchange rate so that the excess demand or supply of foreign exchange resulting from protection is absorbed. As a result, we can expect protection on the whole to leave the current account balance unchanged.

Similar reasoning applies to the aggregate employment argument.[17] The general level of employment and unemployment is almost entirely the result of conditions in the labor market that determine wages and the level of aggregate demand.

Because of the mechanisms just mentioned, increased employment, even if it occurs in the protected industry, is normally offset by reduced employment elsewhere in the economy. Unfortunately, those who lose their jobs because of protection often do not recognize

---

16. If consumers switch toward the purchase of more nontraded goods, the relative price of nontraded goods rises and pulls resources out of both exportables and import-competing industries. As resources shift, exports tend to fall and imports tend to rise.

17. Protection *can* increase employment in the protected industry, although it will normally be at the expense of employment in other industries.

the linkage of their fate to trade policy. In some instances, protection of importers simply leads to exporters' not increasing their sales. Even when export orders are lost because of a somewhat appreciated exchange rate (or because of reduced foreign incomes resulting from protection), normally so many factors affect the fortunes of individual firms that even their top officers cannot accurately attribute causation. But we can normally expect the higher prices of protected commodities that reduce exporters' competitiveness and the diversion of employment from exportable to import-competing industries to offset most, if not all, of the effect increased protection has on employment in a particular industry.[18]

While it is certainly possible that protecting the American automobile industry may "save" American jobs in automobile production, at least in the short run, that does not mean that there are more jobs in total. The new export industries and the industries servicing automobiles create fewer new jobs. The total level of employment and the rate of unemployment are macroeconomic phenomena, determined largely by macroeconomic variables and very little by the level of protection.[19] We can expect protection to shuffle employment rather than to increase it.

Postwar Evolution of the International Trading System

Background. The spice trade with Asia and other exotic trading patterns and routes existed long before the Industrial Revolution. But trade really flourished in the eighteenth and nineteenth centuries, as transport costs fell and Great Britain adopted a policy of free trade. During the latter part of the nineteenth century, other industrial countries followed the British example.[20]

As the Industrial Revolution progressed in the late eighteenth and nineteenth centuries, trade expanded even more rapidly than did

---

18. In addition, as already noted, estimates of the annual costs to consumers of jobs saved are normally several times the annual earnings of workers in protected industries.

19. Under fixed exchange rates countries could export their booms and recessions as demand for other countries' exports fell. In such circumstances one could argue that if the rest of the world were about to suffer a recession, increased protection might buffer a domestic economy from the recession's impact. Under floating rates, even that is a much less pronounced factor.

20. The United States was an exception. It maintained tariffs averaging over 40 percent on dutiable imports (20 to 25 percent on total imports) as late as the 1890s. Those average tariff rates did not fall significantly until the Underwood tariff law became effective in 1913. See GATT (1994, 78, table 1).

real output and living standards. Trade expanded at that rate because the Industrial Revolution increased the variety of goods and services available and hence the potential gains from trade. Moreover, the Industrial Revolution progressed rapidly partly because sharply falling costs of transporting goods from country to country and the "golden age" of relatively free trade among the major European countries provided large gains from trade.[21]

The growth of trade and the increasing integration of the international economy continued throughout the nineteenth century and up to World War I. For the next thirty years, however, the international economy suffered severe dislocations. Perhaps the most dramatic of those was the Great Depression and its aftermath, although the problems of German war reparations, the British difficulty in reattaining pound convertibility under the gold standard, and other strains in the 1920s had prevented the reemergence of a smoothly functioning international economic system. The Great Depression was accompanied, however, by precipitate drops in levels of exports and imports. In turn, virtually throughout the world, living standards fell sharply and dramatically.

One of the intensifiers of the Great Depression was the Smoot-Hawley tariff in the United States, which Congress passed in 1930. Smoot-Hawley raised tariffs to extremely high levels, and other countries in turn retaliated by raising their tariffs and imposing other trade barriers. Those policies were intended to increase domestic employment and production in import-competing industries as demand for exports was falling. Instead, each country's protective response offset others' protection and intensified the Great Depression. Over the next several years, country after country abandoned the gold standard and adopted exchange controls. Finally, the system as a whole collapsed. By 1933 the United States itself abandoned the gold standard.

Not only was the decade one of continuing difficulty in the foreign exchange markets and international trade, but economists and the public alike associated those difficulties with the protectionist measures that had been taken early in the decade.[22] Indeed, the term

---

21. See North (1968) for an account.

22. The United States itself changed policies in 1934 with the passage of the Reciprocal Trade Agreements Act. Then–Secretary of State Cordell Hull was a firm believer in free trade and led the move away from the high tariffs of the Smoot-Hawley regime. The Reciprocal Trade Agreements Act provided for negotiations to reduce tariffs on a reciprocal basis, with a "most-favored-nation" clause in the resulting agreement. MFN clauses had been official policy since 1923, but they assumed additional importance with reciprocal negotiations. The MFN clause, in turn, implied that tariff reductions negoti-

beggar-thy-neighbor came to be used to describe policies that were designed to increase aggregate demand at home by reducing imports (including both raising barriers to imports and competitive devaluations). Those policies were followed by foreign policies that had the same intent and effect. The circle thus created resulted in a severe downward spiral and harmed all.

Planning the Postwar Era. As it became clear that the Allies would emerge victorious from World War II, the Americans and the British led the planning for the postwar international economy. Much of the thinking of economists at that time centered on the urgency of preventing a repetition of the competitive devaluations and beggar-thy-neighbor protectionist policies that were so widely regarded as having intensified (if not having started) the Great Depression.

The architects of the postwar system believed that their challenge was to devise an international system that would prevent individual countries from taking unilateral actions, such as devaluation or increasing barriers against imports, that when countered by their trading partners would result in a mutual worsening of well-being. To that end, the planners proposed the International Trade Organization along with the International Monetary Fund and the International Bank for Reconstruction and Development, subsequently known as the World Bank.[23]

For present purposes, we need not further consider the functions assigned to the World Bank and the IMF, except to note that the underlying philosophy was that the fund would oversee trade and exchange arrangements to prevent competitive devaluations and to ensure an international monetary environment in which an open multilateral trading system could facilitate economic growth in all countries.

To develop an international system that would be immune from the downward spiral that had started with the Smoot-Hawley tariff, the planners of the postwar system proposed that the International Trade Organization oversee conduct with respect to tariffs and other trade barriers similar to the IMF's intended role as a policeman pre-

---

ated between the United States and France, for example, were automatically extended to all other U.S. trading partners with whom such an agreement had been signed. For a history of the negotiations surrounding the structure of the postwar system, see Gardner (1956).

23. Strictly speaking, the World Bank consists of the International Bank for Reconstruction and Development and several other institutions, the most important of which is the International Development Association, the concessional window of the World Bank.

venting competitive devaluations. While world leaders were considering the ITO charter, an executive agreement in 1947 established a framework for international trading relations, the General Agreement on Tariffs and Trade. The intent was that the GATT would govern international trading relations until such time as the ITO came into being. The GATT articles contained many of the key provisions pertaining to trading arrangements that were to be embodied in the ITO. The U.S. Senate never approved the ITO, however.[24] Thus, the GATT continues as the international organization governing trading relations among nations.[25]

The GATT articles set forth principles to which GATT signatories would adhere and provided for mechanisms for dispute resolution among member trading countries. There were three central sets of provisions. The first set governed the trade policies countries would adopt or eschew in trading with other countries. They are discussed further below. The second set established a secretariat that would, *inter alia*, monitor world trading conditions and provide a mechanism for settling disputes between signatories. The third set made the GATT the medium through which countries would negotiate for reciprocal tariff reductions and changes in trading relations.

Principles Accepted by GATT Signatories. As stated in the GATT articles, the fundamental principles on which the GATT is organized[26]

---

24. In the fall of 1950 a press release from the White House indicated that the president did not plan to submit the ITO charter to Congress for its approval, which was tantamount to announcing its demise. The reasons for the failure of the ITO to emerge were several. On one hand, a number of supporters of free trade opposed it on the grounds that the charter had too many exceptions to free trade principles. On the other hand, protectionists opposed the ITO because they believed that it "gave away" too much sovereignty over major issues pertaining to full employment. In addition, the GATT as a functioning institution greatly reduced the need for the ITO. Besides, the president had other, more pressing, items on which he needed congressional action. See Diebold (1952) for an account.

25. Under the Uruguay Round agreement, in 1995 the World Trade Organization (different in a large number of ways from the ITO envisaged under the Havana Charter) supersedes the GATT. The WTO will be responsible for trading arrangements in services as well as goods and will have considerably enhanced oversight responsibilities. See chapter 6 for a further discussion.

26. The GATT charter has many provisions that are important, but not central, to the argument of this monograph. The interested reader can consult Dam (1970) for an excellent exposition of the GATT. An appendix to Dam contains the text of the agreement itself.

include especially nondiscrimination among trading partners.[27] Countries agree to establish their trade regimes without differentiating among their trading partners. They also agree to eschew nontariff border measures, with certain exceptions spelled out in Article XI.[28]

Those two key principles, put together, imply an *open multilateral* trading system. "Openness" refers to the fact that relying only on tariffs implies that all goods may be imported freely, subject only to paying whatever rate of duty is in force. "Multilateral" embodies the notion that countries will agree to, and abide by, the same trading practices with all of their trading partners.

The GATT permits some discrimination among trading partners when a free trade agreement or customs union is reached. The GATT charter also states conditions under which countries may adopt protective measures. Those include cases in which imports cause "severe disruption" (the escape or safeguards clause) and cases in which exporters in foreign countries "dump" their goods on a country's market.[29] Although the provision is not germane to the United States, countries may also depart from GATT rules and resort to quotas to restrict imports in cases of severe balance of payments difficulties. The original GATT charter also contained provisions regarding sub-

---

27. Article XXIV of the GATT permits customs unions and free trade agreements, provided that they apply uniformly to "substantially all" trade and do not increase duties and regulations governing trade with third countries. In addition, a few special provisions, mostly added after the original treaty was signed, permit differential treatment for developing countries. Chief among those is the dispensation permitting developed countries to have preferential (lower) tariff rates on commodities entering their borders from developing countries than the rates applicable to other developed countries.

28. As with nondiscrimination, there are a few exceptions to the rule barring nontariff barriers. They also apply primarily to developing countries. After World War II, European countries and Japan used a balance of payments provision, under which countries could resort to quantitative restrictions if balance of payments pressures forced them to do so. After reconstruction, however, the developing countries chiefly imposed quantitative restrictions, which they justified with the balance of payments provisions. In fact, the GATT charter also has an infant industry exception, but developing countries seem to have found reliance on balance of payments exceptions more accessible, using Article XVIIIB. Scholars increasingly question whether such "special and differential" treatment of developing countries is in their interests. See Wolf (1987).

29. Dumping, and its counterpart, state subsidies, are both practices against which GATT members are entitled to retaliate under the charter. Since the charter provides the legal justification for U.S. administered protection, I discuss it further in chapter 3.

sidies (Article XVI—countervailing duty provisions), although in that article the country providing the subsidy was obliged to "discuss" the subsidy with any party that was threatened with "serious injury" as a result of that subsidy. The intent was to limit subsidization. For years, the United States sought and ultimately secured a stronger subsidies code. In the Uruguay Round, parties agreed to further provisions restricting subsidies, but the United States has subsequently declared its unwillingness to take part in them.[30]

There is a third principle that underlies a great deal of the GATT—"national treatment." Countries have always, by virtue of their sovereignty, regulated various aspects of domestic economic activity if they so chose for such reasons as setting health and safety standards, raising revenue, and providing consumers with information. Under GATT rules (and for economic efficiency), foreign products entering a country's national market may be subject to the same regulations as domestic industries. If, for example, there is an excise tax of 50 percent on all liquor, taxing imported liquor in that amount is consistent with the GATT.

In practice, there are difficulties in drawing the line between "national treatment" and health, safety, or other measures that are protective in effect. Countries have attempted to protect some of their industries by imposing very specific requirements that affect imports[31] but not domestic production or that give domestic producers a significant advantage over their foreign competitors.[32] U.S. automo-

---

30. The reason is apparently the U.S. administration's belief that subsidization of "high-tech" R&D and perhaps other expenditures should be part of its economic policy. See Council of Economic Advisers (1994, 190ff.).

31. To pass health, safety, or other regulations to discriminate against imports is not consistent with the GATT. When issues such as emissions standards are debated, however, local producers normally advocate standards that will give them an advantage over their foreign competitors.

32. An interesting example of "unintended" protection of that type arose in Brazil in the 1960s. A producer of small-engine aircraft believed that he could compete in the U.S. market and applied to the Federal Aviation Administration for certification that his engines met American safety standards. The FAA responded that it was required to inspect any engine-producing factory before issuing a certificate and that it had no funds for sending inspectors overseas. It rejected the company's offer to finance the cost of travel for inspectors and instead suggested that it would accept the results of an inspection done by one of the several U.S. firms that were already certified. Those firms, however, had no interest in helping another competitor gain access to the U.S. market! The American ambassador to Brazil had to intervene to achieve the desired inspection and certification.

bile manufacturers are widely thought to have advocated emission standards that they believe themselves capable of meeting more cheaply than can their foreign competitors, for example.

Despite the difficulty of finding the appropriate dividing line between "genuine" regulatory issues and efforts to use national treatment as hidden protection, the third principle is certainly desirable. The United States has long advocated the principle with respect to foreign investment as well as trade. We shall see in subsequent chapters, however, that many current U.S. trade practices do not honor that principle, because they find foreign firms guilty of practices that are perfectly acceptable and legal for U.S. firms.

The GATT Secretariat. When the GATT articles were signed, a secretariat of the GATT was established, and it has operated ever since in Geneva. The director-general of the GATT is its chief officer.

The GATT council is empowered to establish panels to resolve trade disputes between member countries. Thus, when one member believes that another member has violated its GATT obligations in its trade relations, it may bring a formal complaint to the GATT. A panel is then established to arbitrate the dispute. Although the United States has appealed to the GATT with complaints, there is a widespread belief that GATT panels are very slow and that dispute settlement is therefore largely ineffective. I shall argue in the final chapter that the appropriate solution to that problem is to strengthen the secretariat and the dispute-settlement procedures.[33] Although the United States has used GATT mechanisms for dispute settlement, American trade officials have more often been inclined to resort to bilateral bargaining that weakens the GATT system.

In recent years members of the GATT agreed to inaugurate a "trade policy review" process under which each signatory provides data on its trade policies and the GATT formally reviews them.[34]

Merely requiring a different standard from those imposed by governments in countries in which major competitors are located will make it more difficult for those competitors to sell in "our" market. But it will also make it more difficult for our producers to sell in theirs, with resulting increasing costs for all.

33. Steps to achieve that end are already envisaged for the new World Trade Organization. Under the WTO, a number of changes would be made in dispute-settlement procedures that would mitigate some of the criticisms that have been leveled. Interestingly, opponents of the WTO now argue that the improved dispute-settlement procedures may threaten U.S. "sovereignty." For an analysis of that issue, see Jackson (1994).

34. For the results of the first review of U.S. trade policies, see GATT (1989).

Members hoped that those reports would result in greater transparency of trade restrictions and would thus reduce the extent to which countries could by complexity and obscurity indulge in protectionist practices.

The GATT secretariat is relatively small, with fewer than 200 employees in 1992, compared with more than 2,000 at the IMF and 7,000 at the World Bank. It is also underfunded relative to the World Bank, the IMF, or UN organizations. In part, the GATT's relatively small size derives from the fact that the body is a "secretariat." In part, the secretariat is small because each year it depends on its member countries to approve and fund its budget.

Multilateral Trade Negotiations. At the end of World War II, most industrialized countries still relied on quantitative restrictions and bilateral trading arrangements. The United States emerged with its productive capacity largely intact and was a highly open economy contrasted with most European countries, Japan, Australia, New Zealand, and the developing countries.

Those countries relied on exchange control and even bilateral trading arrangements, in part as a residual from the traumatic 1930s and in part as a consequence of the large demand for foreign exchange (which, at that time, meant almost exclusively U.S. dollars) to obtain needed supplies and equipment for reconstruction. The war dislocated domestic capacities to produce and hence to earn foreign exchange. The United States was virtually the only country with adequate productive capacity. In consequence, the U.S. current account was large and positive, both because countries were running down their assets to purchase needed goods and because the United States was helping to finance reconstruction through the Marshall Plan and other measures.

Tariffs were also high in many countries, as a legacy of the Smoot-Hawley tariff and the beggar-thy-neighbor policies of the 1930s.[35] Bilateral trade and payments arrangements were multilateralized partly as a result of U.S. leadership under the European Payments Union, a component of the European reconstruction efforts financed by the Marshall Plan. As recovery proceeded, quantitative restrictions were also gradually lifted.

Successive rounds of multilateral trade negotiations have taken place since the late 1940s. In the first round in Geneva, tariffs were

---

35. The average U.S. tariff on dutiable imports was 29 percent in 1945 and 20 percent in 1947. It thereafter fell sharply to 14 percent in 1948 under the influence of the first round of tariff negotiations. See GATT (1994, 80).

cut by an average of 21 percent; the remaining duties were on average about half of their level in 1930—the year of the infamous Smoot-Hawley tariff. By the early 1970s, however, scholars could argue that GATT negotiations had such "remarkable success" that nontariff barriers should be the chief concern of negotiators.[36]

In the early rounds the United States, Canada, the European countries, and Japan were the major participants. Bargaining took place between pairs from among this group, with each participant's identifying tariffs it would like the other to reduce, and the other's responding with suggestions as to tariffs that might be reduced in return. Because of MFN provisions, the tariff cuts as negotiated were extended to all members. By the end of the 1970s, the average tariff level among the negotiating countries was about 20 percent of its 1930 level.[37]

In each round of tariff negotiations, once the parties reached agreement, tariffs were "bound" at their new, reduced levels, and the participants undertook not to increase them again unless imports caused "serious injury." Even with serious injury, countries were to "compensate" the trading partner against which a tariff was once again raised by offering other concessions. The GATT provided for the establishment of dispute panels in the event one country declared serious injury and the other either disagreed with the claim or offered inadequate compensation.

One can even argue that some of the new forms of protectionism discussed in later chapters are the result of the success of the GATT negotiations in reducing and binding tariff levels. When countries cannot raise bound tariffs but are under strong political pressures to do something, the temptation to erect nontariff barriers is strong. To a considerable extent, there is a need for response, and a major question is whether that response should be through the actions of individual governments or whether instead it should be through the GATT. That is a topic I address in later chapters.

By any standard, the first quarter century following the establishment of the GATT was the most prosperous in history. The European and Japanese economies not only grew rapidly during the 1950s

---

36. Baldwin (1970, 1) reported that after the Kennedy Round tariff cuts were completed, tariffs on nonagricultural imports subject to any duty at all would average 9.9 percent in the United States, 8.6 percent in the European Community, 10.8 percent in the United Kingdom, and 10.7 percent in Japan. Tariffs were further reduced by almost another 50 percent under the Tokyo Round.

37. Data are from Baldwin (1988, 20, table 2.1).

(when many thought that rapid growth would end once economies reattained their prewar levels of output), but continued their rapid growth into the 1960s and 1970s.[38] Rapid growth provided an environment in which the industrial countries could rapidly liberalize their trade. That liberalization, in turn, stimulated even more rapid growth. Although most of the developing countries' trade policies were increasingly restrictive, even their growth rates were by and large satisfactory as they benefited from the buoyant world economy, although their share of global trade fell from 1950 until 1980. Thus, the open multilateral system under the GATT served the world economy well. By any measure, trade in manufactures among the industrialized countries was increasingly liberalized from the 1950s to the 1980s.

Note, however, that the liberalization of world trade was confined (at least until the 1980s) largely to the industrialized countries and largely to trade in nonagricultural commodities.[39] When the GATT articles (within the ITO charter) were negotiated, the U.S. authorities strongly believed that no agreement could pass that did not leave U.S. agricultural programs intact. Thus, the GATT articles contain a specific provision for barriers to agricultural imports when domestic production restrictions are in place for those commodities.

Despite that provision, U.S. farm policy measures rapidly were found to be in violation of the GATT, as U.S. dairy legislation did not provide for production restraints but did entail restrictions on imports. Subsequently, the United States obtained a waiver from the contracting parties covering its agricultural programs.[40] At that time, Japanese and European agricultural production levels were still relatively low as postwar reconstruction was continuing. Over time, however, European policies under the common agricultural policy and Japanese policies became increasingly restrictive. By 1970, as all Eu-

---

38. Most developing countries achieved rates of growth of per capita income well above their historical averages. In part, those growth rates were realized because of the conditions prevailing in the world economy. During the 1950s and 1960s, however, most developing countries moved counter to the trend toward liberalization among industrialized countries. When the rate of growth of the industrialized countries fell in the 1970s and dropped even more so in the early 1980s, many developing countries found that their former growth rates were unsustainable. The period after 1983 witnessed a number of developing countries' reversing their earlier protectionist policies and beginning to integrate more into the world economy.

39. To be sure, falling transport and communications costs in fact increased the integration of the world economy for all goods and services.

40. See Dam (1970, 260ff.) for an account.

rope, Japan, and the United States were carrying out agricultural policies clearly running counter to the spirit and articles of the GATT, Dam (1970, 257) could write, "It would be difficult to conclude that the GATT's record in the sphere of temperate agricultural commodities is other than one of failure." Indeed, as trade in manufactures has become increasingly liberalized, trade in agricultural commodities has become more distorted. Although official U.S. policy is to insist that Europe and Japan are the culprits with respect to agricultural protection, U.S. law (section 22 of the Agricultural Adjustment Act) instructs the Department of Agriculture to restrict imports of agricultural commodities whenever they will "interfere" with domestic agricultural programs. In 1994, for example, the Department of Agriculture found that imports of wheat from Canada were interfering with the U.S. wheat program, despite the fact that a poor U.S. harvest had been the proximate cause of those additional imports.[41]

One of the key issues the United States raised in the Uruguay Round was the height of protection of agriculture in Europe and Japan. Given the great success of GATT negotiations in reducing trade barriers among manufactured goods, it seems clear that trade barriers for agricultural commodities (and some services) are the most economically costly barriers to trade in the 1990s.

The U.S. Shift from Multilateral Leadership to Aggressive Bilateralism

We have already seen that American leadership was critical to the push for trade liberalization. At the end of World War II, the United States was the only major industrialized country that did not have quantitative restrictions and exchange control governing most of its trade relations. The United States signed and urged leaders of other countries to sign the GATT articles. The United States promoted trade liberalization in most of the European countries under the Marshall Plan and through leadership in proposing and supporting successive rounds of tariff negotiations under the GATT.

Not only did the United States assume leadership in urging the reduction of trade barriers in other countries, but until at least the 1970s, U.S. policy unequivocally supported the principle of free trade,[42] despite U.S. agricultural policy and restrictions on imports of

---

41. *Financial Times*, April 21, 1994, p. 3.

42. In recent years the American labor movement has been highly critical of open trading policies. Until the late 1960s, however, U.S. labor unions supported trade liberalization. See Baldwin (1988, 26–27) for an account.

29

textiles and apparel.[43] In part, that support derived from foreign policy concerns. But, in addition, memories of Smoot-Hawley contributed to general acceptance of a liberalized, open trading regime. Politicians defended such departures from free trade as "exceptions" to the general policy, and the burden of proof lay squarely with those who advocated protection.

Since the 1970s, however, U.S. policy has become increasingly schizophrenic. On one hand, there has been support for successive GATT rounds and other trade-liberalizing measures. At the same time, however, the United States has increasingly resorted to restrictive trade measures both in practice and in rhetoric and is no longer unswerving in its support for multilateralism. In rhetoric much of the discussion has used catchwords such as "free trade but fair trade" to imply that intervention is warranted if other countries are "unfair" traders. In the 1980s U.S. official policy shifted away from unequivocal support for the open multilateral trading system to a "two-track" approach under which support for the GATT would be coupled with measures to enter into free trade agreements with particular countries.

Restrictive measures have included bilateral bargaining on sector-specific and country-specific issues in response to domestic protectionist pressures from individual industries. They have also included increasingly frequent resort to "administered protection" as a means of protecting domestic producers.

The next several chapters of this work trace in some detail the increasing resort to extra-GATT trade practices. We shall see in chapter 3 that the law governing administered protection has been altered in ways that make conditions defining antidumping, countervailing duty, or "unfair trade" practices much broader than they were historically. We shall also see in chapter 4 that bilateral bargaining with Japan, Korea, and other countries has assumed a much larger role in U.S. trade relations than was earlier the case. Finally, I shall argue in chapters 5 and 6 that those practices and the development of free trade agreements have substantially increased the dangers of both trade wars and the gradual shift to trading blocs.

---

43. The Short-Term Agreement of 1955 with Japan was the first agreement restraining imports of textiles and apparel into the United States. Subsequent regulation of textile and apparel imports extended country and commodity coverage. Until the 1980s, however, imports of textiles and apparel rose rapidly, and one could argue that the Multifiber Arrangement had not been highly restrictive. By the mid-1980s, there was considerably more evidence of its "bite" with respect to imports.

Before turning to more detailed scrutiny of those phenomena, it may be useful briefly to consider why American policy has changed. No definitive answer is, of course, possible. In part, practices such as administered protection, once started, have a logic of their own that leads to increased laxity of the restrictive circumstances under which they were initially intended to apply.

At least two major factors contributing to the shift in American policy can, however, be identified.[44] The first relates to the declining relative position of the United States in the world economy. The second concerns U.S. macroeconomic conditions since the early 1980s.

The gradual shift in trade policy roughly coincides with the reduced relative economic importance of the United States. Table 2–1 provides data on world trade. As we can see, trade grew phenomenally. World trade doubled in value terms between 1950 and 1960 and then more than doubled between 1960 and 1970. Trade increased even more rapidly in each of the subsequent two decades despite a much lower rate of inflation in the 1980s than in the 1970s. The rate of growth of trade in manufactures has been more than twice the rate of growth of real world GDP.

The third column of table 2–1 gives total U.S. exports as a share of world trade. At the end of World War II, the United States emerged as the single most economically powerful country. The war-destroyed economies of Europe and Japan had limited productive capacity and large demands for all sorts of commodities that were available only from the United States; the only limits on U.S. exports were American capacity and the financial resources of U.S. trading partners. After that, U.S. exports continued expanding, but the U.S. share of world trade dropped as Europe and Japan completed reconstruction and began growing rapidly. Especially between 1960 and 1980, the U.S.

---

44. It is evident that the shift in policy corresponds to a reduced concern for "global" or systemic issues and an increased concern for narrower domestic interests. Baldwin (1988) described the shift as one from circumstances in which foreign policy considerations were predominant to those in which domestic political interests held sway. While that has certainly happened, it does not explain why the shift began in the 1970s, when national security concerns were still regarded as crucial. The "end of the cold war" could, perhaps, explain an acceleration of the shift to domestic considerations in the 1990s. It is too early to ascertain whether there has been any such acceleration. Indeed, one can argue that domestic considerations of general economic welfare and the public interest call for a return to unequivocal support for the open multilateral system. One can also argue that the drift away from multilateralism and free trade represents a shift toward the increased influence of special interests.

share was falling; although the United States still remained a very large and important trading nation, it no longer was *the* dominant country.[45] Ironically, as the U.S. share of world trade was falling, the importance of trade to the United States was rising. In 1950 exports had constituted only 5.0 percent of U.S. GNP; by 1960 exports were 5.8 percent. They rose to 12.8 percent in 1980, before falling to 9.9 percent in 1990 (Council of Economic Advisers 1992).

Interestingly, U.S. support for the open multilateral trading system was greatest when the United States held unrivaled economic power in the world economy and exhibited considerably less interdependence with the rest of the world than it does today. As the U.S. preeminence has diminished and American dependence on the international economy has increased, one could argue that U.S. interest in an orderly international *system* should have increased. Instead, attention has focused much more on parochial interests in particular industries.

This monograph examines the U.S. shift in interest from an open multilateral trading system to the parochial interests of certain industries. Understanding that shift requires first an understanding of "administered protection," as it has evolved in American trade law and practice over the past two decades. That is the subject of chapter 3.

---

45. The small increase in U.S. share between 1980 and 1990 obscures a large intradecade shift. In the early 1980s the U.S. dollar appreciated relative to the currencies of the major U.S. trading partners, and the U.S. share of world exports fell. In the second half of the decade, the dollar depreciated, and the U.S. share of world exports grew rapidly.

3

Administered Protection

It is the thesis of this monograph that U.S. trade policy has become increasingly schizophrenic. On occasion U.S. policy supports an open multilateral trading system. At other times it relies on bilateral trading relations and uses the rhetoric of "fair trade" as a screen behind which to follow protectionist practices. This and the following two chapters document that proposition. Although the United States has not abandoned its commitment to the GATT (and now its successor organization the WTO), a series of policies, practices, and legislative changes has shifted U.S. trade policy away from almost exclusive reliance on multilateral procedures to much greater reliance on bargaining bilaterally with individual or small groups of trading partners.

Trade Remedy Law and Its Abuse

An open multilateral trading system is one in which all trading nations agree on the "rules of the game." Nations treat all other nations "as the most favored." Under GATT rules, when a country fails to honor its GATT obligations, the aggrieved country may register a complaint with the GATT. Advocates of an open multilateral system would argue that remedies for trade practices in violation of the GATT should be sought through GATT procedures that could, and should if necessary, be strengthened.[1]

By contrast, bilateral trade relations involve bargaining between

---

1. Participants in the Uruguay Round agreed to strengthen dispute procedures as well as to increase coverage of multilateral rules.

the United States and a trading partner (or a few partners) over trade practices. To be sure, there will always be bilateral issues such as the number and location of consulates. But for an open multilateral trading system to operate effectively, the rules of the game must be set forth multilaterally and remedies sought predominantly through an international agency, notably the GATT and the WTO. The United States, as the largest trading nation and a leader in the world economy, could do much to strengthen the system by relying on and strengthening GATT mechanisms, instead of going outside them. When the United States increases its reliance on bilateral measures, it emboldens other countries to follow similar practices. It is no coincidence that, as the United States has increased its use of antidumping and countervailing duty trade remedies, other countries have increasingly resorted to the same measures (Boltuck and Litan 1991a, 6).

American trade policy has increasingly used bilateral bargaining over trade issues. That bargaining has taken place when the American president has met with, for example, the Japanese prime minister to discuss trade practices that the U.S. administration believes are unfair. Such bargaining has occurred when the United States has sought changes in trade practices from the Koreans, the Taiwanese, the Thais, and others in bilateral bargaining over particular issues.

This analysis considers two main parts of the law—the antidumping, antisubsidy (countervailing duty), and escape clause (injury or safeguards) provisions and the unfair trade provisions. The latter pertain to practices that are deemed unfair, but are not within the purview of the GATT articles. The unfair trade practices, under section 301, are used extensively in bilateral bargaining. I discuss them further in chapter 4.

Here, I focus on antidumping and countervailing duty provisions. In recent years they have been the "protectionists' instrument of choice."[2] They have provided protection directly, and industry representatives have filed them to induce the U.S. administration to negotiate other relief measures, such as voluntary export restraints, which I discuss in chapter 4.

It is necessary to start with a brief description of how U.S. trade remedy laws operate. The laws are, by and large, consistent with the

---

2. Until the 1970s, escape clause actions were more frequently used. Under those provisions, a finding of injury from imports must be made. For positive antidumping or countervailing duty findings, the injury test is that there must have been "material injury" to the industry from imports—a far weaker test than that applied under the escape clause. See Boltuck (1993) for an analysis of the application of the injury test.

GATT, although as we shall see, the way in which they are administered gives them protectionist content well beyond the intent of GATT provisions. And, regardless of whether they are consistent with GATT principles, the manner of their administration has conferred protection on American firms because of the deterrence value of the mere threat of antidumping or countervailing duty litigation. Indeed, plaintiffs have filed those two actions with the clear intent of pressuring the U.S. executive and foreign governments to agree to a voluntary export restraint or other protectionist measures.[3]

Over the years, U.S. administered trade laws have become increasingly restrictive in a number of ways and thus have acquired increasingly protectionist overtones. Indeed, many have termed the operation of those laws "administered protection."[4] Threats of administered protection have induced trading partners to accept other bilateral measures, such as voluntary export restraints, in preference to the trade remedy alternative. By the mid-1980s, the United States was the largest single user of administrative trade law remedies.[5]

Under the GATT articles, countries are entitled to maintain safeguards against surges of imports that might otherwise result in severe economic dislocation. In such a case injury to domestic import-competing producers is the criterion against which cases are judged under escape clause or safeguards provisions of domestic legislation and GATT articles. Also under the GATT, countries may maintain antidumping procedures to protect against foreign firms' pricing be-

---

3. For example, petitions accusing Colombian rose growers of dumping were filed five times between 1986 and 1994. The penalties imposed were within the 1 to 5 percent range. Harassment of the growers was widely believed to be a motive behind those filings, despite the small penalties imposed (Passell 1994, C2). In an industry such as cut flowers, where inventories cannot be kept (and where, therefore, the alternative to current sales is to throw away the flowers), the notion that it is "dumping" to sell below cost is bizarre. Passell noted that the domestic industry was urging comparison between the prices at which Colombian roses sell in Europe (in very small quantities) and the prices at which they sell in the (large) U.S. market. Evidently, Colombian rose growers were considering abandoning their European sales to avoid that threat. Ironically, the consequence would be to increase Colombia's exports of roses to the United States.

4. See Rugman and Anderson (1988) for a Canadian perspective on those trade remedy practices. Rugman and Anderson, as well as others, maintain that a major Canadian motive for seeking the U.S.-Canada Free Trade Agreement was to enable Canadian producers to avoid the effects of U.S. antidumping, countervailing duty, and escape clause actions.

5. See Finger and Nogues (1987) for an account.

low normal value[6] and may impose countervailing duty rates on foreign companies whose costs are lowered by virtue of a direct or an indirect (upstream) subsidy. The use of subsidies and the sale of products at dumping prices are generally regarded as unfair trade practices.

U.S. trade law has long contained provisions for trade remedies when industries or the government establish injury or unfair practices—either government subsidies or private firms' selling at "too low" a price with consequent injury to the domestic industry. Over time, however, the restrictive impact of those laws has increased. Congress has weakened criteria for finding in favor of unfair trade practices, and restrictions on presidential discretion in interpreting findings have increased. In addition to those legal changes, U.S. firms have increasingly resorted to administered trade remedies.

Moreover, as we shall see, U.S. practices have now extended well beyond antidumping, countervailing duty, and escape clause provisions. In instances in which Congress deems that other countries' practices are unfair, it has mandated trade remedies bilaterally, despite the fact that the trading partner's practices are not inconsistent with the GATT.[7] That mandate provided the basis on which the U.S. trade representative has investigated other countries' practices with respect to intellectual property protection. The most egregious example of this was Super 301,[8] a provision that instructed the USTR to examine partner countries' trading practices and to list their unfair trading practices. The USTR was to brand countries with such trading practices as unfair traders and to impose punitive retaliatory trade measures in the event that the trading partner did not abandon those practices. Super 301 is perhaps the quintessential bilateral trading practice. Unlike antidumping, countervailing duty, and escape clause administration, which is, at least on the surface, consistent with the GATT, Super 301 and related measures are inherently bilateral and

---

6. The criteria in Article VI of the GATT are: selling at less than the comparable price in the exporting country; in the absence of such a price, either selling at a price below that in which the item is sold in a third country or selling below "cost of production," including a "reasonable addition for selling cost and profit" (Dam 1970, 400). According to Article VI, "due allowance" must be made for different conditions in different markets.

7. The wording of section 301 also *permits* the U.S. administration to proceed in a wide variety of circumstances in which it may deem practices to be unfair, even if not GATT-inconsistent.

8. President Clinton reinstated Super 301 in the winter of 1994. It is included in the bill the Senate passed on December 1, 1994, to ratify the Uruguay Round agreement.

operate blatantly outside the GATT framework (Hudec 1990). I discuss Super 301 and other bilateral trade measures in detail in chapter 4. In this chapter I explain the American administered protection process, the threat of which has often been sufficient to give the United States considerable bargaining power in bilateral disputes.

Antidumping and Subsidies Provisions of Administered Protection

Origins. Like many other countries, the United States has trade laws governing situations in which firms in other countries sell at dumping prices or receive subsidies from their governments. The fact that such laws exist is not in itself evidence of protectionism, and the laws apply equally to all countries, although antidumping and countervailing duty cases are heard on a country-by-country basis.

Administered protection of antidumping and countervailing duty provisions is inherently bilateral because each petition for protection specifies a particular country or countries where firms engage in the specified unfair trade practices. Insofar, however, as administered trade remedies are authorized under the GATT and are designed to provide relief from practices that all countries have agreed are unacceptable, they need not be protectionist in effect.[9] In the 1950s and 1960s, antidumping and countervailing duty legislation provided for relief, and there were occasional cases in which tariffs were imposed to offset findings of dumping or of injury. The number of such occasions was relatively small, however.

Starting in the 1970s, administered protection became increasingly important, and the legal provisions for a finding that foreign firms had dumped or received subsidies were significantly relaxed. Many of the ways in which the law is administered imparted a substantial bias against foreign producers, to the point where many practices that could lead to the finding that a foreign firm had, for example, dumped are perfectly legitimate for domestic firms. As the conditions under which positive findings for antidumping or countervailing duties were eased, foreign governments became increasingly willing to negotiate alternative measures to avoid the erratic and often punitive nature of antidumping and countervailing duty findings. Among the changes that led to a higher probability of an affirmative finding were the transfer of the responsibility for investigating the

9. Note, however, that some subsidies are not deemed unacceptable under the GATT but are countervailed nonetheless.

37

foreign firms' costs from the Treasury Department to the Department of Commerce.[10]

Within GATT rules, individual countries are permitted to take actions to safeguard their domestic industries under specified circumstances. In the United States the escape clause was the main national instrument for appealing for protection from unfair foreign competition until 1974. American firms appealing for relief from imports had to show not only that imports had increased, but that they had constituted a major source of injury to the domestic industry. In most instances it was difficult to prove that imports were a sufficiently important source of injury to obtain a positive finding.[11]

In the Trade Act of 1974 the injury standard under which relief would be granted was changed to "material" injury, which was consistent with GATT criteria, although a weaker hurdle than earlier. Under that legislation, those appealing for protection had only to show that foreigners engaged in unfair trading practices—either selling below the cost of production in antidumping cases or receiving subsidies in countervailing duty cases—and that the result had been material injury. Few firms availed themselves of the 1974 legislation, and Congress further weakened the injury test in 1979.

After the injury test was weakened, firms and industries rapidly shifted from appealing on the basis of section 201 (escape clause) and instead began using section 301, including antidumping and countervailing duty provisions. Table 3–1 gives data on the number of cases filed, affirmative findings, and total number of actions in effect in the 1980s and early 1990s for the United States.

By the late 1980s, the United States had filed more antidumping and countervailing duty cases than any other country in the world save Canada! From 1986 through 1988, the United States had filed 124 antidumping, 34 countervailing duty, 7 escape clause, and 14 other trade investigations. During the same period the European Community had filed 95 antidumping, 2 countervailing duty, and 29 other cases; Australia (earlier the champion in terms of number of cases and again in the early 1990s) had filed 97 cases; Canada had filed 224 antidumping, 12 countervailing duty, and no other cases; and

---

10. The Department of Commerce is naturally closer to the business community and is generally regarded as much more sympathetic to the claims of U.S. firms regarding the unfair nature of their foreign competitors' practices than was the Treasury Department.

11. Under GATT rules, "compensation" had to be arranged with trading partners whose imports had caused the injury when tariff reductions had been negotiated as part of multilateral tariff bargaining.

TABLE 3–1
ESCAPE CLAUSE, ANTIDUMPING, COUNTERVAILING DUTY,
AND SECTION 301 CASES BY YEAR AND FINDINGS

Panel A. Section 201 (Escape Clause) Cases

Period	Number of Cases	Number Receiving Relief	Outstanding Affirmative Actions
1975 to 1980	44	8[a]	n.a.
1981 to 1985	15	4[b]	n.a.
1986 to 1990	3	0	n.a.
1991 to 1992	1	0	n.a.

Panel B. Antidumping Actions

Year	Number of Cases	Provisional[c] Relief	Actions Final[d]	Outstanding Affirmative Actions
1981	15	14	5	85
1982	51	59	48	n.a.
1983	19	35	10	52
1984	46	69	33	104
1985	61	65	28	112
1986	63	68	25	122
1987	41	95	40	151
1988	31	35	22	167
1989	25	65	29	198
1990	24	37	17	196
1991	52	47	17	209
1992	24	88	16	n.a.

Panel C. Countervailing Duty Cases

Year	Number of Cases	Provisional Relief[c]	Actions Final[d]	Outstanding Countervailing Duties
1981	7	5	3	48
1982	75	46	9	n.a.
1983	35	34	23	53
1984	22	17	4	56
1985	60	39	21	86

(Table continues)

TABLE 3–1 (continued)

Year	Number of Cases	Provisional Relief[c]	Actions Final[d]	Outstanding Countervailing Duties
1986	43	24	17	76
1987	11	16	16	89
1988	13	9	10	88
1989	8	11	8	91
1990	6	5	4	86
1991	8	7	4	70
1992	4	43	2	n.a.

Panel D. Section 301 Cases

Year	Number of Cases	Result of Trade Negotiations[e]	
		Liberalization	Retaliation
1980	2	–	–
1981	–	–	1
1982	1	2	–
1983	1	2	–
1984	1	–	–
1985	9	3	1
1986	9	3	1
1987	3	1	2
1988	15	–	–
1989	4	7	–
1990	3	1	–

a. Of the forty-four escape clause cases filed, there were seventeen negative findings, but of the remainder, twelve received no relief, and seven received adjustment assistance or income support. Only eight cases ended with tariff increases or quotas.

b. Of the remaining eleven cases, nine were negative decisions, and in two cases trade adjustment assistance coordination was ordered.

c. Relief includes both provisional measures and definitive duties. Since there are lags between the time a case is filed and the time a decision is reached, the yearly totals do not reflect the outcome of the same cases as are reflected under filings. In addition, one petition may initiate several investigations.

d. Includes both definitive duties and price undertakings.

e. These characterizations are from Low (1993). Cases in which the effect of the negotiations was indeterminate have been excluded.

SOURCES: Low (1993, tables 4.4–4.7) and USITC (1993).

developing countries as a group had filed 75 antidumping cases (Bol-tuck and Litan 1991a, 5). In 1990, 1991, and the first half of 1992, the United States had filed 52 antidumping and 62 countervailing duty cases: the total for the entire world was 175 antidumping and 237 countervailing duty cases. The *Financial Times* (December 15, 1992, p. 15) estimated that average tariffs in the U.S. manufacturing sector were 23 percent (compared with a nominal level of 6 percent) if account was taken of antidumping and countervailing duty actions in force.

During the 1980s there were 64 investigations of Japanese practices, 60 of Brazilian, 43 of Canadian, 311 against EC countries, and a total of 752 antidumping and countervailing duty cases (Boltuck and Litan 1991b, 4). Of those 752 cases, 350 were filed against foreign exporters of iron and steel products, 85 against chemical producers, 61 against food processors, and 21 against textile and apparel producers. The steel industry is certainly the champion filer of complaints against foreign competitors, and it has used the threat of those complaint filings to obtain voluntary export restraint agreements and now to pressure for an international steel agreement.

Antidumping orders had become an important component of American protectionism by the end of the 1980s. In 1980 the U.S. government had 84 outstanding antidumping orders, and by 1990 it had 197 outstanding orders. Moreover, the percentage of American imports covered by antidumping orders rose from 3.43 in 1980 to 9.59 in 1990.[12] Worse yet, antidumping duties tend to be higher than MFN duties. The average duty imposed in antidumping orders in 1990 and 1991 was 55.5 percent, compared with the average MFN duty of 14.4 percent on the same imports (Anderson 1993, 114). From the viewpoint of many foreigners, by the mid-1980s American administered protection had become at least as much a trade barrier against imports into the United States as American tariffs.[13]

---

12. American antidumping orders can remain in effect for a long time period, whereas many countries have automatic sunset provisions. Australia, for example, leaves antidumping duties in effect for only three years. Of the 197 antidumping orders in effect in the United States in 1990, 46 had already been on the books in 1980. The oldest was an order against cement from the Dominican Republic that dated back to 1963. See Anderson (1993) for details.

13. Below I provide an estimate of the average height of tariffs under administered protection measures taken in 1990 and 1991. The concern of many foreigners goes beyond the height of tariffs imposed, however. They point to the uncertainty engendered by the possibility of petitions filed under U.S. trade law and the costs of defense.

Antidumping and Countervailing Duty Procedures. Few would quarrel with the notion that there should be some procedures available in the event that a foreign country's exports are sold uneconomically, although there is some presumption that consumers should welcome cheaper imports. *Uneconomic* normally means below the *marginal* cost of production. Economists would question, however, how often profit-maximizing firms sell below marginal cost. Unless firms expect to drive competitors out of business by selling below cost and thereby gain monopoly power, it makes no sense for a private firm to sell below marginal cost.[14]

On that criterion, any firm, domestic or foreign, that sold below marginal cost with the intent of monopolizing the market should be prosecuted. Indeed, American antitrust laws enjoin American producers from selling below marginal cost (predatory pricing). Many forms of price discrimination, which takes advantage of monopoly power, are also illegal under U.S. antitrust law. From the viewpoint of rational resource allocation and economic efficiency, the criteria for anticompetitive behavior should not depend on the nationality of the firm in question.

As we shall see, however, the standards applied to foreign firms in antidumping cases differ significantly from those applied to firms within the United States. In other words, firms located abroad could be engaging in behavior that would be perfectly legal (and economic) for firms located in the United States and yet find themselves subject to antidumping or countervailing duty action.[15] Moreover, they might be selling well above marginal cost and still be found guilty of dumping.

The procedures used in investigating antidumping cases can be costly to foreign firms and represent a potentially significant deterrent to entry into the U.S. market.[16] Indeed, the threat of filing a petition has been sufficient in many instances for foreign firms to reach a price understanding to raise their prices to avoid antidumping litigation.

---

14. As in the case of semiconductors, it can make sense for a firm to sell below "current" marginal cost if by increasing production volume, costs will fall faster. Only in industries in which there is rapid learning could that be the case.

15. Indeed, it is worse than that. The seller of goods into the United States could be found to have received governmental subsidies and thus be subject to countervailing duties, even if American firms received even greater subsidies!

16. See Nam (1993) for an analysis of costs to Korean firms.

Other studies (Boltuck and Litan 1991b; Bhagwati and Patrick 1990) have well analyzed those aspects of administration of trade remedy laws. They require only brief review here. Turning first to procedural aspects, *any* American firm can file a petition with the U.S. Department of Commerce to seek relief from unfair foreign practices. Once the petition is filed, there are two steps. First, the Department of Commerce must determine whether there has been unfair pricing, and if so, what the margin of dumping (the percentage of unfairness) is while the USITC investigates enough to ascertain whether there is a reasonable likelihood of injury. If its finding is positive, the Department of Commerce ascertains whether there is a reasonable basis for a preliminary finding of unfair practices and provides a preliminary estimate of the antidumping margin. If the Commerce Department and the USITC have positive findings in the first stage, the second stage completes the investigation, and the Commerce Department makes a final determination. If that finding remains positive, the USITC imposes a duty (in the proportion of the dumping margin) on imports that are not priced above the fair price.[17] But even at the end of the first stage, duties are set. Moreover, U.S. importers do not know the extent of their liability when they are importing during the investigation: when imports enter the United States, importers must post a cash deposit of bond equal in amount to the magnitude specified in the antidumping order. But administrative reviews by the International Trade Administration of the Department of Commerce can increase the required payment and cover all entries of the preceding year. The uncertainty as to the magnitude of the liability has been regarded as an additional and serious penalty of antidumping orders. It would be understandable if American importers were unwilling to source their goods from countries where antidumping orders are in effect, because there is no way of knowing in advance what the total costs of imports will be.

Once a petition has been filed,[18] the Department of Commerce sends a notice to the accused parties to inform them of the allegation and provides them with a questionnaire, which is over 100 pages long. As Murray (1991, 34) reports, data requested include:

> specific accounting data on sales in the home market (and possibly to third countries), data on sales to the United

---

17. The interested reader can find more details in Murray (1991).

18. A firm or groups of firms may file a petition, and the Department of Commerce may also self-initiate. In theory, a firm filing the petition is filing on behalf of an industry; in practice, a firm's petition is normally accepted unless other firms in the industry actively oppose it, as sometimes happens. See Murray (1991, 28).

States, data needed to adjust arm's-length market prices to net ex-factory prices (that is, packaging costs, shipping costs, selling costs, distributor and other middleman costs, adjustments for taxes and duties on imported inputs, and adjustment for exporter's sales prices, international shipping costs, tariffs in the United States, distribution costs in the United States and any costs of adding value in the United States).

Foreign firms are given sixty days from the time the Department of Commerce sends the notice to respond. They must respond in English in prescribed machine-readable format on diskettes and must provide all information requested, usually including detailed data on every sale to the United States for at least a six-month period. If accounting practices in the firm's country differ, the firm is nonetheless required to respond according to the standards prescribed by the Department of Commerce. In itself, the adjustment of books to alternative accounting standards can be costly and time-consuming.

Without recounting more of the procedure, it may be noted that a U.S. agency is peremptorily summoning responses from a foreign firm, which in itself can be a subject of resentment. Moreover, for small firms in countries such as Taiwan, where regular bookkeeping practices may not yet be established and where in any event English is not the language, the demands for data can be overwhelming.

Should the foreign firm fail to respond within the sixty days, or if the information supplied is incomplete or otherwise deemed "unverified," the Department of Commerce is empowered to use alternative information, which is normally the information supplied by the plaintiff, whose incentive is surely to overestimate the foreign competitors' costs.

Once the sixty-day period is over, the Department of Commerce weighs the evidence and issues a preliminary finding. If that finding is positive (as it is in the vast majority of cases), a temporary duty is placed on the offending imports, and the foreign exporter must place a deposit against all exports to the United States until the USITC makes the final determination. Often, at that stage, importers will choose to seek alternative sources rather than put themselves at risk for unknown amounts pending the final determination (Murray 1991, 32).

While the request for data and the sixty-day time limit in themselves constitute a unilateral action with respect to a trading partner, procedures used to evaluate whether dumping has occurred are even more questionable. The legal criteria are those of Article VI cited above. Establishing whether the U.S. price was below the foreign market price entails using sales price data provided by the firm. For U.S. sales, however, the Commerce Department rules out any high prices (on the argument that an average price should not take into account extraordinary sales and that one sale should not be used to subsidize another), whereas for foreign sales the department rules out any unusually low prices (on the grounds that selling at an unusually low price in the foreign market does not excuse it in the U.S. market). The Commerce Department then compares the averages of the remaining price data for sales in the United States and sales in the home market.[19]

In at least two ways a foreign firm could sell goods at identical prices and yet be found guilty of selling at a lower price in the United States than at home. First, the timing of sales might vary. For example, in a period of rising prices, sales to the United States might be in the third quarter of the year but have been negotiated with the supplier in the second quarter, given lags in shipping. Sales in the home market, however, might be recorded at prices at time of sale in the third quarter. Thus, the Commerce Department would in fact be comparing the second-quarter sales prices in the United States with third-quarter sales prices in the home country. Second, the rejection of low and high observations, respectively, from foreign and American selling price data could lead to an erroneous finding of guilt. In principle, there might also be instances of systematic quality differences such that the average recorded sales price for the home market was higher than that for the foreign market.

The Department of Commerce is by law required to provide a positive finding whenever the foreign market value (either in the home country or in a third country) is above the U.S. price by half a percentage point or more. That is sufficiently small so that the biases in comparison, noted above, could lead unambiguously to a finding of dumping, even if the foreign firm had priced identically and above cost in its various markets.

If price data are not available for comparison (as, for example, when a factory has been established that sells all its output to the U.S. market), then the Commerce Department is by law instructed to "construct" cost as a basis for comparison. Despite the biases built into the price comparison procedures described above, they are nonetheless probably smaller than the biases in the constructed cost case.

The Commerce Department uses several questionable proce-

---

19. There are also technicalities as to how the U.S. sales price is to be determined, but they are not relevant for purposes of the present analysis. See Murray (1991) for a description.

dures to construct costs. First, the department is required by law to use "best information available." When foreign firms fail to respond within sixty days, the best information available is usually taken to be that in the petition from the American group seeking protection (Murray 1991, 34). Second, the department uses average rather than marginal costs. Third, the department includes an eight percentage point margin as a minimum to cover overhead and profit.[20]

Thus, there are any number of ways in which a foreign firm could be following normal business practices, similar to those American firms follow, and yet be found guilty of dumping. Price comparisons may be biased because low prices in the exporter's home market are not included while high prices in the U.S. market are excluded. If costs are constructed, the margins used, the allocation of costs among joint products, and the use of data provided by complainants can all bias the outcome.

International Objections to Administered Protection

Other countries' representatives have protested against the current practices and procedures in American antidumping and countervailing duty cases. In summing up the GATT review of U.S. trade practices in 1992, the chairman noted that other countries' concerns included: "the application of antidumping and countervailing measures, particularly the uncertainty, harassment and costs caused for foreign competitors" (GATT 1992, 4).[21] The *Economist* (December 7, 1991, p. 30) noted that "the threat of antidumping procedures, along with the thousands of countervailing duties on imported goods, create an impossibly hostile climate for overseas exporters."

American administered protection has caused considerable resentment abroad. We shall see in the next chapter that even Canada and Mexico, despite NAFTA, are not exempt from the uncertainties and other difficulties associated with administered protection. Other countries, especially some developing countries, are adopting U.S. laws for their own protection against dumping. As currently adopted

---

20. Only two of the fifteen largest American companies had an 8 percent margin in 1989 (*Economist*, December 7, 1991, p. 30).

21. The chairman also singled out "unpredictable customs procedures," "use of managed trade practices," and "trigger provisions" among thirteen U.S. trade practices to which there had been objections (GATT 1992, 4–5). The U.S. representative "recognized participants' concerns over unilateral actions by the United States. However, many areas in which Section 301 action had been taken were not currently covered by multilateral rules" (GATT 1992, 6).

and administered, American trade remedy law permits the abuse of procedure for protectionist purposes at least as much as it prevents genuine dumping of the sort that economists believe is harmful.

Review of the cases under which antidumping duties have been assessed makes the plausibility of the dumping argument even more suspect. Three glaring instances illustrate the point. The first was when firms in Taiwan, Korea, and Hong Kong were found to be dumping sweaters in the U.S. market (despite the fact that they were restrained in the quantities they could export by the quotas assigned under the Multifiber Arrangement). Incredibly enough, the USITC ruled that there had been injury, and the Commerce Department found that firms in Hong Kong had been dumping by a margin of 5.88 percent, those from Korea by 1.3 percent, and those from Taiwan by 21.38 percent (Dunne 1990, 7).[22]

A second smaller, but equally telling, case concerned cement from Venezuela. It well illustrates the ways in which antidumping procedures can be used. In the case of Venezuelan cement, prices Venezuelan exporters charged in the Florida market were about the same as those American firms charged. U.S. cement producers claimed, however, that the Venezuelans were selling cement in the Florida market (which is geographically far enough away from other U.S. sources so that other U.S. producers could not compete) at a price below that in the Venezuelan market. The *Economist* (November 2, 1991, p. 64) noted:

> The cement case is just the latest example of how arbitrary, and unfair, America's antidumping laws can be to foreign firms—not to mention American consumers. . . . In a recession, when companies are making little or no profit, injury is easy to prove. . . . The Venezuelans claim that the case against them is a bid by big, vertically integrated American cement and concrete companies to stifle competition in the Florida market. The idea is to deprive Florida's independent concrete producers, who use cement as a raw material, of their supplies. . . . Because cement is generally cheaper in America than abroad, other would-be cement exporters could be equally vulnerable to antidumping action. . . . Excluding all imports could raise cement prices in Florida by a

---

22. The U.S. Court of International Trade overturned the finding of injury in August 1992, and the USITC reversed its ruling in December of that year (*International Trade Reporter*, November 25, 1992; *Journal of Commerce*, December 4, 1992). The industry association, in filing the case, had claimed dumping margins ranging from 13 to 94 percent for Korea, 44 to 190 percent for Taiwan, and 25 to 115 percent for Hong Kong.

third, according to a recent study, forcing consumers, businesses, and local governments to pay an extra $664m over the next five years.

U.S. cement producers filed and won a similar antidumping suit against Mexican cement producers. In this example, it seems clear that the the finding was based on average, and not marginal, costs, and that American firms would have been found equally guilty during periods of recession.

Yet a third case concerned "industrial wiping cloths" (shop towels) exported from Bangladesh. A U.S. textile firm first filed a countervailing duty complaint that Bangladesh was subsidizing the export of those cloths. But the USITC found that the export subsidy was equivalent to .02 percent of selling price, and de minimis, and rejected the case. The U.S. petitioner (Milliken) then petitioned under antidumping provisions, stating that all Bangladeshi exporters had made net losses in 1990. In fact, all those producers had been in a start-up stage in 1990. In addition, Bangladesh's exports were restricted under the Multifiber Arrangement. Despite those considerations (and the fact that Bangladesh exports were $2.46 million contrasted with estimated Milliken sales of $2 billion), the USITC found that the imports of rags from Bangladesh were injuring the U.S. textile industry (Lash 1992a).

U.S. producers have used antidumping and countervailing duty provisions not only as protectionist deterrents to foreign exporters but also as means to secure other forms of relief from imports. Industries' threats to file petitions have on several occasions prompted the administration to seek voluntary export restraints (automobiles, machine tools, and ball bearings, to name just a few), to impose trigger prices (steel), or to take other measures in an effort to avoid administered protection processes when the administration considered the consequences undesirable on grounds of foreign policy, economic relations, or other factors.

Recently, a dozen firms in the U.S. steel industry demonstrated the potency of the antidumping and countervailing duty measures and their role in promoting voluntary export restraints and other protectionist measures. The industry sought to have VERs or other protectionist measures strengthened. When that failed, the steel firms filed a veritable flood of petitions. By the summer of 1993, nineteen countries' steel industries faced antidumping margins averaging an estimated 36 percent, with the highest (against Brazilian and British producers) being 109 percent. The government found that an additional twelve countries had subsidized steel production enough so that duties ranging between 1 and 73 percent were imposed (*New York Times*, June 23, 1993, pp. C1, C18). Ironically, the *Financial Times* (January 29, 1992, p. 13) noted that many of the items subject to duties were those that carried high profit margins.

Sometimes administered protection backfires against those using it most. SCM, a producer of typewriters, has long been known as one of the most blatant users of administered protection, especially against its Japanese rival, Brother. Partly in response to concerns about future suits, Brother established a factory in the United States, while at about the same time SCM invested in offshore production facilities. Brother then reversed roles with SCM by filing a petition against imports from SCM on the grounds that it was dumping typewriters from its offshore plant in the U.S. market (*New York Times*, August 12, 1991, p. 1).[23] Among other things, that case vividly illustrates one of the fundamental questions that should be of concern in U.S. trade law: who is the "United States" and who are the foreigners? Is it location of economic activity (in which case Brother was the "American") or ownership that determines nationality? And, for that matter, why do the rules depend on nationality, especially if a level playing field is the stated concern?

Conclusions

The manner in which U.S. trade law remedies are administered gives them protectionist content beyond what might reasonably be defended on economic grounds. To a considerable degree, those administrative procedures are not mandated by law, but are subject to executive branch interpretation (Boltuck and Litan 1991a, 14ff.). Those procedures clearly have a bias against importers and in favor of domestic producers. As the antidumping and countervailing duty tests have become easier relative to the injury component of escape clause actions, American firms seeking protection from imports have increasingly used those provisions. Moreover, other countries are beginning to adopt them (Boltuck and Litan 1991a, 6–7). Thus, they will increasingly come to be used against American exporters.

The willingness of foreign governments to negotiate VERs and other measures to avoid antidumping and countervailing duty actions most dramatically demonstrates that foreign exporters fear findings and penalties associated with those actions. Therefore, antidumping

---

23. For much more detailed analyses of section 301 and its effects, see the entertaining account in Bovard (1991a) and the analyses in Bhagwati and Patrick (1990) and in Boltuck and Litan (1991b).

and countervailing duty actions have become weapons to be used in bilateral trading relations, an issue I discuss further in chapter 4.

There would appear to be only two possibilities as to the future evolution of administered trade. Nations could agree on an international code for "competitive" practices, presumably under the aegis of the GATT and the WTO. Under such a scenario, countries would harmonize their competition laws or at least give national treatment to foreign firms under their own competition law. In that case practices that are deemed unfair if done by foreigners would also be deemed unfair if done by national firms. That might be a satisfactory multilateral solution to the problem.

Under the second scenario, an increasing number of other countries might adopt administrative procedures similar to those of the United States. Doing so would greatly increase the possibilities of retaliation, counterretaliation, and disruption of the world trading system and would further undermine the multilateral trading system. That process is already underway. Such a trend should cause Americans to reconsider current practices of administered protection. Trading nations should adopt the multilateral solution before the increasingly unilateral treatment by other countries leads to retaliatory actions that will inevitably disrupt the trading system.

4

Bilateral Words and Deeds

American policy, as officially stated, has been to support the open multilateral system through the GATT and its successor the WTO, while pursuing closer trading ties with "like-minded trading partners" through regional arrangements. Simultaneously, the United States has enacted legislation instructing the USTR to deal bilaterally with countries over a number of issues of concern to the United States, and the U.S. administration has negotiated bilaterally with other countries both as mandated by Congress and as seen appropriate to ward off congressional protectionist measures. While U.S. policy pronouncements stress the commitment to an open multilateral trading system and the lack of barriers to imports into the United States, in practice the United States maintains a number of trade barriers on a number of items with political sensitivity, and many foreign trading partners question the U.S. commitment to the multilateral system.

We saw in chapter 3 that the United States has come to use administered trade remedies with increasing frequency and with reduced standards for affirmative findings that permit the United States to impose duties. While those remedies, as administered, are inherently somewhat protectionist, the United States uses them as a weapon in bargaining bilaterally with other countries. In this chapter I discuss some of the bilateral practices that have increasingly emerged in American trade policy.

By "bilateral" I mean those trade policies and practices that the United States carries out on a country-by-country basis. Some refer to those actions as "unilateral," in the sense that the United States acts alone. But a "unilateral" action is one that a single country under-takes with respect to one other country, a group of countries, or the whole world. For example, lowering a tariff or other trade barrier vis-à-vis all other trading partners outside of GATT multilateral tariff negotiations would be unilateral.

For purposes of this chapter, *bilateral* will refer to those trade policies and actions that the United States directs toward specific countries in the context of one-on-one negotiations or bargaining. An example of what is not and what is bilateral may prove useful. In the early 1980s the United States unilaterally imposed sugar import quo-tas without formally consulting or negotiating with trading partners. The decision affected all countries exporting sugar to the United States, and the United States decided and announced the size of each country's quota. There was no reported bargaining.[1] The action was thus unilateral. When, subsequently, the United States bargained with the Philippines over trade issues, one aspect of that bargaining could have been the size of the Philippines' sugar quota: actions such as that are bilateral.

Chapter 3 mentioned that some bilateral relations are inevitable and desirable over trade issues. In recent years, however, much of the U.S. posture has shifted toward demanding trade policy changes from trading partners in bilateral negotiations and confronting coun-tries individually with respect to their trade practices. As we shall see below, while some of those demands are not inconsistent with the GATT, others are more questionable. In many instances the U.S. de-mands have caused a trading partner to increase U.S. access to its market at the expense of a third country.

Moreover, as I shall argue in chapter 6, the net impact of U.S. practices with respect to administered trade remedies, bilateral bar-gaining, and fostering regional trading arrangements has at a mini-mum been to detract from the GATT, and, more recently, from the inauguration of the WTO and to increase trade tensions with individ-ual partners.

---

1. The imposition of sugar quotas would appear to contravene the GATT, and to be sure, it is inconsistent with GATT articles. As noted in chapter 2, however, the United States had earlier received a waiver for its agricultural trade practices and could therefore reinstate sugar quotas that had been used until 1974. The United States went further in 1981, however, and reinstated country-specific import quotas. GATT rules require that any such measure be undertaken among GATT members in an equitable manner. In fact, the United States refused to extend quotas to Nicaragua, which won a case against the United States in the International Court of Law. See Krueger (1990, 195) for an account.

This chapter first demonstrates the unilateral and bilateral patterns into which U.S. trade policy has fallen. To that end, I shall document how the United States has used the threat of administered protection in bilateral negotiations, review some of the sectoral issues that have been subject to bilateral bargaining, consider Super 301 provisions, and evaluate Special 301 and issues of intellectual property rights. Then, to demonstrate how those bilateral actions play out against particular trading partners, I shall trace some aspects of bilateral relations for two individual trading partners, Japan and Korea. A concluding section will evaluate the net effects of those bilateral trade actions. I shall argue that, despite some visible market-opening that may have resulted from those negotiations, the gains have been smaller than might at first sight appear. Indeed, those negotiations have unnecessarily circumvented and hence weakened the multilateral trade institution. Furthermore, the potential for misunderstandings and damage to the international trading system has been greater than is widely recognized. In chapter 6 I shall also argue that the U.S. use of the trade policy instrument to achieve a wide variety of objectives not only undermines the multilateral trading system, but also runs counter to broader foreign policy, as well as trade, interests.

Bilateral Threats of Administered Protection

The United States is a large trading nation. As such, its trade is generally much more important to its trading partners than is their trade to the United States.[2] Not only do many of our trading partners have a larger share of their production in exportable industries, but the share of their trade that is with the United States is usually significantly larger than the U.S. share of trade with them. Between Canada and the United States, for example, the asymmetry of the relationship is pronounced. Over 70 percent of Canada's exports and imports are with the United States. Moreover, exports and imports each constitute over 20 percent of Canada's GDP, so that Canadian exports to the United States account for over 14 percent of Canadian GDP. By contrast, U.S. exports to and imports from Canada each account for less than 20 percent of U.S. trade, and trade constitutes

---

2. Relations with the United States are also important to many countries for other reasons. During the cold war, strategic considerations were probably paramount for many countries. Undoubtedly, the Japanese sensitivity to American pressures can be accounted for in part by the importance of trading relations, but security issues and the Japanese reliance on the American defense umbrella also played a role.

12 to 14 percent of U.S. GDP. Hence, U.S. exports to Canada are 2 to 3 percent of GDP—highly asymmetric.

In and of itself, however, the fact that trade is more vital to U.S. trading partners than to the United States does not confer bargaining power. Because U.S. tariffs are bound under the GATT, resort to the credible threat of administered protection has provided a means by which U.S. trade officials can bargain bilaterally with and impose their will on their foreign counterparts.

The threat value of filing petitions for administered trade remedies is clearly substantial. Not only does the possibility of administered protection serve as a barrier to imports, but it provides a bargaining tool: the United States essentially informs one or more foreign governments that unless appropriate action is taken, countervailing duty and antidumping remedies (or worse through congressional action) will ensue.

Note that the possibility of administered trade remedy permits the U.S. administration to engage in a "good cop, bad cop" game. The administration can profess its commitment to free trade (which may be genuine), while pointing to Congress as a protectionist body that will impose legislated administered trade remedies—presumably against the will of the executive—unless other actions are taken. We shall see below, in discussing sectoral issues, that our trading partners agreed to voluntary export restraints for both automobiles and steel following the threat of administered protection.

Bilateral Trade Relations on Sectoral Issues

Negotiations with individual countries over sectoral issues have covered a large number of economic activities. In some instances efforts have been made to induce the trading partner to remove or reduce trade barriers on certain products exported by the United States. In others, concern has centered on the trading partner's exports to the United States.

The instruments most frequently used have been voluntary import expansion agreements and voluntary export restraints. This section reviews the mechanisms of those two types of agreements and then considers three sectoral agreements—on automobiles, steel, and textiles and apparel.

Voluntary Import Expansions. Issues of market access have arisen with a large number of countries. U.S. officials have publicly asserted that U.S. bilateral measures are intended to "open" trade, which, they claim, is preferable to taking measures to restrict trade.

A number of criticisms can be leveled against voluntary import expansions. Irwin (1994, 3) concludes:

> VIEs are not an appropriate response to foreign trade practices that are allegedly unfair. When such practices can be identified, direct measures to remove or to mitigate them should be undertaken. When such practices cannot be identified, VIEs should also be avoided: because they are so arbitrary, they lack a plausible economic foundation and risk promoting, not competition, but the formation of cartels. VIEs are inherently discriminatory trade measures. . . . The slight probability that they might sometimes produce good results must be set against the far greater probability that they will bring harm.

In addition to those criticisms, scholars contend that VIEs are often discriminatory[3] and that the GATT, rather than bilateral bargaining, is the appropriate forum for getting international agreement on acceptable practices. Moreover, when bargaining takes place under the GATT, the practice is for a country to offer to remove some of its own trade barriers in return for reduced barriers by its trading partners. In the case of VIEs, most bargaining has consisted of U.S. demands and a foreign response, with little attention to any U.S. quid pro quo.

Critics have noted that the use of VIEs undermines the political economy of the GATT process. Once VIEs are negotiated without a quid pro quo, U.S. exporters, believing that they can achieve their objectives through direct pressure on trading partners, will be less inclined to support multilateral negotiations that move the political equilibrium closer to free trade.

American trading partners, moreover, point out that the efforts of U.S. officials to achieve VIEs (and therefore market opening) take place at the same time as other U.S. trade policies restrict imports into the United States. They therefore consider the rhetoric of market opening as somewhat hypocritical. Below I review a very prominent VIE, that negotiated in the semiconductor case with Japan. That case illustrates many of those points.[4]

---

3. Irwin (1994, 8, 10–11) cites the cases of Canadian eggs and American auto parts. In the egg case, the U.S. complaint (that Canada was too restrictive in importing eggs from the United States) was resolved by a doubling of the Canadian quota allocated to the United States. In the case of auto parts, the Clinton administration has been explicit that its criterion will be the increase in the share of American parts in Japanese consumption.

4. The Clinton administration has insisted, however, that Japan accept "quantitative" indicators of its market opening with respect to a number of other imports. To date, the dispute has not been resolved, although it was

Voluntary Export Restraints. When industry representatives seek protection, they are normally singling out imports as a source of their difficulty. One would anticipate that—in keeping with the nondiscriminatory principle underlying the GATT and also the principle that a country is always better off importing from the cheapest foreign source—industry representatives would attempt to secure protection from *all* imports. In fact, administered protection itself is designed as an instrument to be used against the imports of individual countries. Partly for that reason, industries seeking import relief have generally sought measures aimed at individual countries.[5]

Examining the instances in which relief has been obtained produces a number of conclusions. First, the relief is high-cost for American consumers and imposes a substantial toll per job "saved." Second, since measures are bilateral, imports from third countries have generally constituted a major "problem" for the industry seeking protection. Third, other U.S. producers lose from protection because they pay higher prices than their foreign competitors. Finally, protected U.S. industries have "benefited" far less from the protection than they anticipated.[6] While U.S. protectionist measures are as harmful for U.S. interests as are foreigners' protectionist actions for theirs, the costs of U.S. protection are higher because American rhetoric and bargaining remain based on the conviction that the United States is somehow much less tainted by other countries. In addition, the costs are higher because of the size and importance of the United States in the multilateral trading system.

U.S. producers have forced the negotiated "restraint" of imports into the United States of a number of items, including footwear, television sets, machine tools, and stainless steel flatware. By one estimate, there were sixty-nine voluntary export restraints in effect in 1989, not counting those under the Multifiber Arrangement (Low 1993, 76). For present purposes, however, an account of three of the most visible and important sectors in which the United States has sought import restraints—automobiles, steel, and textiles and apparel—will suffice to illustrate the main points.

---

announced that those indicators could consist of a wide variety of measures—not simply the level of imports.

5. There have, however, been a number of instances in which U.S. producers have filed petitions for import relief on antidumping or countervailing duty grounds against a number of countries at the same time. The steel industry's petitions have been most comprehensive in that regard.

6. See Hufbauer and Elliott (1994) and the evidence summarized in Krueger (forthcoming).

A "voluntary" export restraint is a negotiated arrangement under which an exporting country undertakes to restrict its exports to the market of its trading partner. Responsibility for restricting imports is therefore left to the exporting country, which may then allocate export rights through administered measures, auction rights to sell in the U.S. market, or assign an industry association to ensure compliance with the agreed-upon level of export restraint. There are few recorded instances of auctioning export rights to individual firms in countries subject to VERs.[7] Quite aside from the effects on U.S. consumers of restricting levels of imports under VERs, one may question the wisdom of negotiating VERs. In the absence of auctioning the export rights, VERs either enhance the authority of foreign bureaucrats (when U.S. rhetoric asserts the desirability of market solutions) or enable, or indeed require, industry representatives to collude.[8]

Automobiles. In the late 1970s and early 1980s, the American automobile industry experienced a significant reduction in demand. Imports were increasing and, in addition, the recession sharply reduced the total demand for automobiles.[9] Although the United Auto Workers had first pressed for protection after the recession of 1974, the downturn of 1980 led to a sharp cutback in production, and representatives of the auto industry sought protection by filing an antidumping case. To the surprise of many, the USITC found that imports were not a major cause of the industry's difficulties; the commission concluded that output had fallen primarily because of reduced domestic demand.

When the industry failed in its effort to obtain administered protection, congressmen introduced a number of bills that would have severely restricted imports of automobiles. The ensuing complex sig-

---

7. In Hong Kong rights to export apparel to the United States are auctioned and freely sold in the market.

8. It has also been claimed that the increased price for which the exporter can sell the product in the U.S. market has sometimes increased foreign exporters' profits, thus strengthening them financially for further competition with U.S. producers. That concern has been expressed about both the Japanese automobile industry and the semiconductor industry. Many observers believe that the high prices for which semiconductors sold after the semiconductor agreement in 1986 enabled Korea to enter the semiconductor market so successfully. Note that under the VER, the Japanese could not even increase sales to ward off competition from the Koreans or other producers.

9. Recall that Chrysler had been experiencing difficulties and in 1979 was granted a U.S. government loan. See Nelson (forthcoming) and Reich and Donahue (1985) for a discussion of the background to the VER episode.

nals between the U.S. administration and the Japanese government ended when the Japanese government announced in May 1981 that it would restrict exports of automobiles to 1.68 million units per year.

The profits of Japanese automobile makers consequently rose, and Japanese producers were naturally not unhappy with the VER. When President Reagan stated in 1985 that there was no need to renew the automobile VER, the Japanese government astonished Americans by announcing that it would maintain the automobile VER (Low 1993, 115). The quantity of imports permitted increased to 2.3 million units in 1985 but was cut to 1.65 million units in 1992. Low (1993, 115) attributes that cutback to the Japanese government's belief that protectionist pressures (during the American recession) were once again mounting and that "voluntary" reduction could avoid an even more restrictionist outcome.

This voluntary export restraint was of questionable GATT legality (Jackson 1988). It also had high economic costs for American consumers because it added an estimated $2,000 to the price of an imported automobile. It is estimated that the total costs to Americans were $160,000 per year per job (temporarily) "saved" (Crandall 1984).[10]

In light of the difficulties of the American automobile industry in the late 1980s and evidence that costs were high relative to its Japanese competitors, it seems clear that imports were a problem for the American industry precisely because it had failed to achieve needed cost reductions and improved quality control. A solution to the problem would therefore require addressing those underlying issues, rather than protecting the industry from imports. One can even argue that efforts by the auto industry to secure protection and the Japanese VER may even have slowed down the response of the U.S. industry to the necessary adjustments and hence harmed the industry.

Be that as it may, we should note that the United States imposed no VER on imports of automobiles from other countries. Indeed, during the period of the Japanese VER, Hyundai, a Korean producer, began exporting automobiles to the United States. Automobile producers in Europe must have also been delighted with the VER on Japanese cars.

Quite aside from the costs of export restraint on American consumers and the unintended consequences for other automobile producers, the Japanese VER fundamentally subverted the open multilateral trading system in three important ways. First, U.S. tariffs

---

10. That estimate applies to the first years of VERs. Hufbauer and Elliott (1986, 259) provide estimates ranging from $105,000 to $241,000 per job saved, depending on the year and the assumptions made.

on automobiles were already bound under the GATT, and the VER was blatantly an end run around that binding. Second, by restricting imports from Japan but not from other countries, the United States penalized the low-cost producer. Third, the VER was discriminatory in that it singled out Japan.

Steel. As noted in chapter 3, the steel industry was the most blatant user of the threat to impose administered protection; it filed more than 200 petitions in 1982 and numerous petitions on other occasions (Low 1993, 103–107). Moore (1994, 2) reports:

> The standard steel industry approach is to use or threaten to use the relatively nondiscretionary antidumping or counter-vailing duty processes as a lever to obtain an agreement that provides some degree of price stability in the U.S. market. First, the steel industry (usually with close cooperation from firms and the USW) files massive petitions under U.S. trade remedy laws, especially antidumping and countervailing duty petitions. Simultaneously, congressional supporters of the steel industry introduce GATT-inconsistent quota legislation. Before the quasi-judicial AP process can grind to completion and prior to final votes on the legislation, the Executive Branch will urge the steel industry to accept a negotiated settlement with foreign exporters, usually a VER. This sequence was repeated with slight variation in 1969, 1977 and 1984. In essence, the rules-based administered protection procedures have been utilized as a credible threat to force political settlements onto steel disputes.

Until the late 1980s, each successive round of petitions was concluded with an agreement under which foreign governments voluntarily restricted their steel exports to the United States.

In the late 1970s Japan informally began restricting its exports of steel to the United States (despite the presence of a restrictive trigger-pricing mechanism under which Japanese—thought then to be the low-cost producer—prices were deemed to represent the lowest prices that were not dumped). Even so, dollar appreciation and the recession of the early 1980s led the steel industry to seek protection through antidumping and countervailing duty petitions against European producers. The Department of Commerce found that thirty-eight European steel producers had relied on subsidies, and the European Community negotiated a VER with the United States at the end of 1982 that reduced bulk steel exports by 9 percent. That measure removed the threat of additional U.S. import duties.

Without using antidumping or countervailing duty arguments as a rationale, in 1989 the industry pressured President Bush to extend steel VERs for two and a half years. Instead, the industry argued that foreign producers had an "unfair" competitive advantage.[11] Japanese, EC, and other representatives strongly rejected those allegations. An EC statement suggested that the U.S. industry's problems were the result of "the inability of the major integrated producers to compete successfully with the more efficient" U.S. minimills, which had emerged as successful competitors to "big steel" in the 1980s. A Japanese spokesman asserted: "American steelmakers should look inward to discover the real cause of their problems. . . . Japanese and other overseas steelmakers are not the cause of U.S. overcapacity, the destructive price competition for market share among integrated mills and mini-mills, or the recession" (Low 1993, 106). Low reports that both the European Community and Japan regarded the antidumping and countervailing duty threats as "tantamount to trade harassment" (106). He notes that the VER-negotiated quotas had not been filled.

Hufbauer and Elliott (1994, 20) estimate the 1993 loss in welfare attributable to steel countervailing duty and antidumping actions as $59 million, although the loss to consumers was estimated at $1,035 million. They estimate that the cost to the American consumer per job saved was $84,000 in 1993. One side effect, the magnitude of which cannot be well estimated, has been the induced loss of competitiveness for American exporters whose supply of steel has been at prices higher than their foreign competitors'.

All analysts point to the large integrated U.S. producers' high cost structure and inability to adapt as major factors contributing to their reduced profits and loss of competitiveness. Clearly, the entrance of the minimills had played a significant role in steel's difficulties. Nonetheless, U.S. producers used antidumping and countervailing duty procedures (and potential congressional legislation) as threats to secure VERs from foreign suppliers. Those VERs imposed costs on American consumers, saved some jobs but at a very high cost, antagonized Europeans, Japanese, and others who observed the emergence of minimills and the high cost structure of the "big steel" companies, benefited countries not covered under the VERs, and disadvantaged American exporters using steel as an input. It is arguable that protection did little for the large integrated steel producers.

Again, third-country phenomena undermined the effectiveness

---

11. The Department of Commerce made final determinations of dumping margins that ranged from 3.7 to 109 percent and subsidy margins as high as 73 percent. In July 1993, however, the USITC ruled that imports of all hot-rolled and most cold-rolled steel products had not caused material injury (Hufbauer and Elliott 1994, 19).

of the agreement from the viewpoint of the U.S. steel industry, as Brazilian, Korean, and Mexican producers began exporting to the U.S. market. In response, the Reagan administration undertook to negotiate more global arrangements under which steel imports were to be reduced to 18.5 percent of U.S. domestic consumption. Interestingly, some restricted suppliers were unable to meet their quotas by 1987 as worldwide demand had increased. Canada, however, was unrestricted, so imports of steel from Canada rose.[12]

For present purposes, however, there are five key points. First, VERs involved bilateral trade negotiations, using the threats of antidumping and countervailing duty as bargaining counters. Second, those negotiations were clearly and obviously protectionist in intent. Third, third-country effects made bilateral VERs in any event an unwieldy instrument. Fourth, once VERs had started, they had a tendency to spread both in geographic and in product coverage. Finally, U.S. trade policy was clearly guided more by steel industry pressures than by any concern with an open multilateral trading system or even the welfare of all U.S. producers taken together.

Multifiber Arrangement.[13] The auto and steel industries began the postwar era as exporters, lost their shares of export markets, and ultimately switched to import-competing industries seeking protection. By contrast, the textile and apparel industry has sought protection almost continuously since the mid-1950s. Interestingly, protection started in 1955 with the inauguration of a short-term agreement for a VER with Japan.

The history of the Multifiber Arrangement, among other things, vividly illustrates the importance of multilateral aspects of trade. The first step was in 1956, when the United States "persuaded" Japan to impose a VER on textile and apparel exports.[14] In 1961 that arrange-

---

12. See Low (1993) and Moore (1994) for more detailed accounts.

13. Under the Uruguay Round agreement, the Multifiber Arrangement is to be dismantled over a period of ten years. Not only will tariffs replace quotas, but tariff levels will be brought down. The discussion here describes the situation as it has persisted over the recent past. If dismantling of the Multifiber Arrangement proceeds at the agreed-upon rate (and it almost surely will if the United States fulfills its obligations under the Uruguay Round agreement), that will serve as one of the most valuable and fundamental achievements of the Uruguay Round.

14. According to Low (1993, 197), the United States sponsored Japanese entry into the GATT. Some other countries invoked the GATT grandfather clause to continue their existing restrictions against Japanese exports, but the United States could hardly do so while at the same time sponsoring Japanese entry into the GATT. "Persuasion" to impose a VER resolved the problem.

ment was superseded by a short-term arrangement that contained restrictions covering sixty product categories and sixteen countries.[15] That arrangement was designed to include other importers, as well as the United States.

When the Multifiber Arrangement emerged full-blown, negotiations first took place between the importing countries and the exporting countries to agree on global quotas; thereafter, bilateral negotiations decided on quotas item by item.

Since the first short-term arrangement, problems have arisen as new entrants to the industry locate in countries not covered by the agreement. Those entrants are sometimes financed by direct foreign investment from a producer in a country in which quotas constrain additional exports. Also, problems have arisen as exporters have on occasion been accused of sending their products through other countries to circumvent quota restrictions.[16]

Since 1961, each agreement has been succeeded by one that has increased both product and geographic coverage. The initial agreement concerned only cotton goods, but textile producers early recognized that synthetic substitutes also had to be regulated if the VERs were to have any significant impact. As new entrants have begun exporting, they have been brought into the arrangement. By 1993, the Multifiber Arrangement had forty-one signatories, counting the European Community as one, and thousands of product categories. Cotton, cotton blend, wool, synthetic fibers, linen, ramie, and vegetable fiber products are all covered under Multifiber Arrangement IV, which went into effect in 1986 for an intended period of five years, but which was extended when the Uruguay Round was not completed on its original timetable.

Because of the global nature of trade in textiles and apparel, the Multifiber Arrangement was incorporated into the GATT framework, despite the fact that it contravenes virtually every GATT principle. Essentially, developed and developing countries negotiated a framework agreement under GATT auspices. That agreement set indicative rates of growth for world trade in textiles and apparel. Countries then bilaterally negotiated individual quotas for each item. Virtually all developing countries that export any sizable quantity of exports of

---

15. The short-term arrangement was short term only in the sense that it was succeeded in 1962 by the first long-term arrangement!

16. In 1994 a significant dispute with the Chinese authorities centered on the U.S. contention that Chinese-produced apparel was being transshipped to the United States through third countries. See Council of Economic Advisers (1994, 222).

textiles and apparel have become subject to Multifiber Arrangement restrictions, while industrialized countries do not restrict trade among themselves.

Such a procedure is highly discriminatory. It imposes quantitative restrictions with little regard to the competitiveness of producers. Restrictions are set based on differences in price and without regard to the normal GATT standards of injury. Implicitly, those restrictions favor developed country production in other developed countries' markets at the expense of (often lower cost) developing countries' exports and encourage new entrants (as well as developed countries) at the expense of established producers.[17] And for developing countries, there is little competition with regard to costs and economic efficiency: market shares are established via bargaining based primarily on historical shares with some allowance for room for newcomers.[18]

Undoubtedly, the Multifiber Arrangement constitutes the single most costly aspect to U.S. consumers of U.S. protection. Hufbauer and Elliott (1994) have estimated that in 1993 liberalizing the Multifiber Arrangement in textiles would have generated a consumer surplus gain of $3.2 billion, while liberalization in apparel would have provided a gain of $21.2 billion. They estimate that the cost per job gained in that sector was $144,751 in 1990 (1994, 15, 88–89). Despite

17. Those producers whose countries have experienced rapid economic growth are able to retain their market shares longer than would otherwise be the case, however. For example, the rise in Korean real wages would have rendered the Korean textile and apparel industry less competitive more rapidly than it in fact became had it not been for the existence of Multifiber Arrangement quotas. A delayed phaseout of production and exports from rapidly growing, newly industrialized countries has probably harmed their growth, as well as that of those whose production could have been expanded at lower cost. Ironically, producers in countries such as Korea became supporters of the continuation of the Multifiber Arrangement, as they benefited from it. Consequently, opposition to the Multifiber Arrangement was restricted to new entrants among developing countries.

18. To be sure, initial determination of the quota is based on earlier performance, so there is some competition at that stage. Despite the existence of the Multifiber Arrangement, antidumping petitions were brought against exporters of womens' knit sweaters in Hong Kong, Taiwan, and Korea. As already mentioned, it is hard to imagine why an exporter who is restrained in the amount he can sell would find it to his advantage to sell at "dumping" prices in the restricted market. Nonetheless, antidumping tariffs of 5.8, 21.4, and 1.3 percent were found for the three. To impose a 20 percent margin of difference between tariffs applicable to imports of competing producers in two locations is startling.

its high costs, the Multifiber Arrangement has not satisfied the industry, whose problems in any event originate at least as much from being an unskilled, labor-intensive industry in a period of rising real wages as they do from import competition.

The Multifiber Arrangement also well illustrates why a multilateral approach to trade problems is essential. Efforts to contain imports on an individual country basis are bound to be ineffective, because of the highly elastic supply of textiles and apparel from other existing and potential producers. If imports of several types of textiles or apparel are restricted, imports of other types increase. Ramie, for example, was introduced as a fiber in the 1980s precisely because it was not subject to restriction under the Multifiber Arrangement. As imports of ramie increased, the Multifiber Arrangement coverage had to be extended. Moreover, in the current context of a continuing Multifiber Arrangement, unilateral liberalization would prove far more difficult than multilateral liberalization. If the United States were unilaterally to liberalize trade in textiles and apparel, those producers excluded from European markets would compete in the U.S. market. If, instead, multilateral liberalization is carried out as anticipated, the necessary adjustment for any given importing country's industry will be greatly reduced.

Super 301

We have already seen that Congress authorized section 301 procedures—investigating unfair trading practices of foreign exporters into the United States market—in addition to antidumping and countervailing duty legislation. The United States used those measures with increasing frequency in the 1980s in bilateral bargaining, in which it threatened antidumping or countervailing duty action to induce trading partners to accept VIEs or VERs.

The Omnibus Trade and Competitiveness Act of 1988 extended section 301 of the Trade Act of 1974 to broaden considerably the scope of the unfair trade procedures and took it well beyond measures that are consistent with the GATT in principle. In particular, Congress instructed the USTR to take an inventory of other countries' unfair trading practices, to identify those practices, and then to identify countries engaging in those practices as unfair traders in a report to Congress by the end of May of each year. The USTR was then, on a timetable laid forth in the law, to negotiate with the designated country to achieve the removal of those practices. That provision was immediately dubbed Super 301 to distinguish it from the provisions that permitted the USTR to identify a particular unfair practice and to negotiate over that. The 1988 trade act also instructed the USTR to take retaliatory action against imports from the named country (or countries) in the event that the USTR could not negotiate for removal of the named practices.[19]

Super 301 is inherently a bilateral measure, and there are clearly many circumstances in which it is not consistent with the GATT. It has threat value, the same as antidumping and countervailing duty measures, but it can be applied in instances in which there has been no prior agreement among countries and without any U.S. quid pro quo.

Super 301 came in for severe criticism for a variety of reasons. I have already described its blatant bilateralism and circumvention (or worse) of the GATT system and GATT obligations. In addition, Congress passed that provision when multilateral trade negotiations were underway in the Uruguay Round, which made the circumvention of the GATT more damaging. The 1988 act did not require an executive department or an agency to evaluate the importance of a trade practice to the American economy, and it established no process to insulate decisions regarding Super 301 from protectionist pressures. Finally, Super 301 was arrogantly unilateral in ways that were highly irritating to many U.S. trading partners.

Turning first to GATT consistency, the timetable mandated for the USTR under Super 301 was demonstrably faster than GATT procedures so that, even if GATT procedures were available for dispute settlement, they could not be used effectively.[20] Moreover, the United States was to be the sole determiner of "unfair trade practices."[21]

---

19. Special provisions were made for examining other countries' treatment of intellectual property rights (Special 301, discussed below) and their practices with respect to telecommunications and government procurement.

20. Hudec (1990, 142) pointed out that the United States itself violated the section 301 deadlines in its dealings with the GATT in six cases in the two years before Hudec's article. Hudec noted that "the United States is guilty of worse sins than the ones it complains about in others" (143). Among his conclusions were that "[t]he heart of the problem is that the law is based on an outrageous premise—namely, that the commands of Section 301 do not apply to the United States. . . . Besides being wrong in itself, the one-sided premise has also corrupted the substantive content of the new Section 301" (152).

21. See chapter 6, where I further discuss workers' rights and efforts to insist on a code under the WTO. There is a legitimate basis for concern that insistence on workers' rights could be used as a pretext for protectionist measures against developing countries with a comparative advantage in products using relatively low-cost, unskilled labor.

Nothing in the law precluded retaliation that would be inconsistent with GATT principles. Thus, Super 301 allowed the United States to find a trading partner "guilty" of unfair trade by virtue of inadequate workers' rights and to retaliate by raising GATT-bound tariffs against the trading partner.[22]

The second objection, that Super 301 was inappropriate when the Uruguay Round negotiations were under way, was raised not only in academic circles, but even by the director general of the GATT, Arthur Dunkel, who asserted that Super 301 was an obstacle to the Uruguay Round and suggested that the measure should be substantially weakened (USITC 1990, 5). The GATT secretariat identified Super 301 as the single trade policy initiative that "could have the biggest impact on the multilateral trading system and on the Uruguay Round." Many countries including those in the European Community, Australia, Israel, and the countries named as unfair traders (see below) voiced formal criticisms.

The third objection, that the USTR is exposed to protectionist pressures and that there is no independent assessment of the relative importance of the practices cited to the U.S. economy (or even U.S. interests more broadly) speaks for itself. Given the ability of special interest groups to pressure for their own self-interest, the absence of any mechanisms to permit the USTR to distance himself or herself from those pressures is striking.

That Super 301 is blatantly unilateral was evident in any number of ways. Perhaps the most telling is that the criterion by which the success of the USTR in obtaining relief from "unfair" foreign practices was judged was the extent to which U.S. exports—not global exports—to the country increased (USITC 1990, 4). But Super 301 also put the USTR in a position of being able to decide what trade practices would be deemed unfair (without international agreement), to accuse other parties of those practices, and in effect to try the country according to his or her own rules.

Under Super 301 the USTR singled out Japan, Brazil, and India as "unfair traders" in the first mandated report to Congress. Before that report, however, the USTR's staff was bargaining strenuously with its counterparts in Korea, Taiwan, and other U.S. trade partners

---

22. In a widely cited article, Hudec (1990, 140–41) raised the question as to the GATT-consistency of Super 301 and noted that there *might* be a case for "justified disobedience" to international law under two conditions. The first condition is that the law is clearly not working as it should. The second condition is that the disobedient party must itself clearly adhere to the rules it is attempting to enforce.

to wring concessions from them to escape the Super 301 label. The staff offered no quid pro quo in the sense of trade liberalization. Indeed, the inducement to liberalize, which Korea, Taiwan, and many other countries treated very seriously, was to *avoid* being labeled an unfair trader by the United States.

Fortunately for the multilateral trading system, Super 301 was not renewed when it expired at the end of 1990. Its passage and use, to that date, represented the zenith of U.S. unilateral actions in the trade arena and provided the ultimate demonstration of the American turn away from the GATT toward unilateralism. Had Super 301 continued to be in effect, it is doubtful that the Uruguay Round of trade negotiations could even have been concluded.

By the winter of 1994, however, bilateral trading relations with Japan—discussed in more detail below—had deteriorated under the Clinton administration's pressure for "quantitative targets." In March 1994 President Clinton reinstated Super 301 by executive decree. He insisted that the bilateral trade balance with Japan, and even the magnitude of Japanese imports of individual items, were legitimate subjects for bilateral bargaining. He threatened retaliation (presumably punitive tariffs) if Japan did not address, to the satisfaction of the United States, the "unfair trading practice" of a large bilateral trade imbalance.[23]

Those trends represent an alarming departure from the principles of the open multilateral trading system, and reinstatement of Super 301 augurs poorly for the future of multilateralism. I shall further discuss that issue in chapter 6.

Intellectual Property Rights

U.S. trading partners found Super 301 objectionable because of its unilateralism and because the United States could designate countries as "unfair" trading partners for policies and practices that they had not considered unacceptable in the GATT. The Omnibus Trade and Competitiveness Act of 1988 contained another provision, often referred to as Special 301. Declaring that the protection of intellectual property rights vitally affected U.S. international competitiveness, Congress mandated that the USTR identify countries that "deny adequate and effective protection of intellectual property rights, or deny fair and equitable market access to U.S. persons that rely upon intel-

---

23. The USTR immediately threatened retaliation in the Motorola cellular telephone case; that, however, arose out of a regular section 301 case and was simply convenient to invoke as a first step in the retaliatory process.

lectual property protection."[24] The USTR was to name those countries that most negatively affected the United States through their practices and that did not enter into "good faith" negotiations or make "significant progress" in negotiations to protect intellectual property rights (Low 1993, 64).

When the law was passed, the United States had already succeeded in placing intellectual property rights on the Uruguay Round agenda—the appropriate way to secure multilateral agreement on issues relating to intellectual property rights. Special 301, however, was blatantly bilateral, not only in instructing the USTR to bargain bilaterally, but in insisting on an international code of behavior that had not been agreed on internationally.

The USTR followed that mandate by investigating and reporting on the status of protection of intellectual property rights by all U.S. trading partners. The USTR then reported to Congress that all countries' intellectual property rights laws were deficient and that she was bargaining with each country individually to make the changes deemed necessary (USTR 1992, 266). Instead of naming priority countries, the USTR created a priority watch list and a watch list. Taiwan and Korea, among others, were on the priority watch list. By April 1992, eight countries and the European Community were on the priority watch list, and twenty-three countries were on the watch list.

In discussing bilateral relations with Korea, we shall see that intellectual property rights were one subject of contention. When Korea altered its intellectual property rights regime, the United States received special treatment that generated protests by a number of other U.S. trading partners.[25]

Low (1993, 93) summarizes the impact of Special 301 well:

> [D]esignated foreign countries have been reluctant to cooperate, resenting the unilateral, intrusive, and accusatory flavor of the designations. . . . [T]his particular adventure in aggressive trade policy has not been a success. Its trade policy benefits have been minimal, and it has generated gratuitous political tensions. Its high profile and its automaticity

---

24. The 1988 legislation also significantly weakened criteria for relief under section 337 of the Tariff Act of 1930, which covered intellectual property rights.

25. The Omnibus Trade and Competitiveness Act of 1988 also provided that the USTR identify priority countries for bilateral negotiations on market access for telecommunications and government procurement. The European Community and Europe were named as priority countries under the telecommunications provision. Government procurement has been the subject of disputes with Japan and the European Community.

have militated against constructive dialogue on specific problems.

Bilateral Bargaining between Countries

By definition, bilateral trading relations concern direct negotiations between two trading partners. The negotiation of steel and auto VERs involved the United States and the Japanese for both industries and the Koreans and Europeans for steel. Multifiber Arrangement negotiations involve each of the many developing countries allotted quotas under the arrangement in a bilateral bargaining framework.

But bilateralism has extended far beyond isolated bargaining sessions on import rights into the U.S. market and the exchange of VERs to avoid antidumping and countervailing duty procedures. Regarding many aspects of trade, U.S. "demands" have been made on a country-by-country basis and have extended well beyond negotiations over restricting exports to the United States.

Bilateral negotiations on some subjects have taken place with almost all countries: intellectual property rights is a prominent case in point. Until the Uruguay Round, the GATT agreement contained little pertaining to intellectual property rights, and the United States took the position that infringement of intellectual property rights was harmful to the U.S. competitive position in the world economy. In country after country, U.S. negotiators have insisted that their counterparts secure stronger domestic laws regarding intellectual property rights.[26]

On other subjects, particular countries have been targeted, often under pressure from a U.S. industry. One such case, which has received a great deal of publicity, is the regulation of cigarette advertising, in which the United States has demanded market access and advertising rights in a number of countries (notably Thailand and Korea). As those rights to advertise extend beyond what firms may

---

26. Much of the political pressure for intellectual property rights protection has emanated from the pharmaceutical industry. The industry's position is that it cannot afford to spend on the development of new drugs only to have them copied in countries where there is inadequate or no patent protection. It can be argued that intellectual property protection is in the self-interest of developing countries in the course of their development; but there are certainly cases where it is against their interest. It is not entirely clear that exporters of patent-protected products will gain in all circumstances in which intellectual property rights are protected, and there are circumstances in which imposing intellectual property rights protection in a poor country will diminish world welfare. See Chin and Grossman (1990).

advertise in the United States, many people have noted the disparity in U.S. concerns between the health of their own nationals and the sales of American-made cigarettes in foreign countries.[27]

To trace all of those contentious negotiations would require volumes and serve little purpose.[28] The purpose of this section is to illustrate, through two examples, how the various trade remedy laws, bilateral negotiations, VERs, and other U.S. trade policies have in fact affected trade relations. I consider trade relations between Japan and the United States and those between Korea and the United States.

Note that U.S. trade law does require the United States to use GATT processes when GATT agreements are applicable. In most instances bilateral negotiations have taken place regarding aspects of the trading partner's policies or practices that the United States deemed to be outside the GATT. The new WTO will encompass many of those issues. I shall argue in chapter 6 that the appropriate American policy response at this juncture should be to eschew the bilateral route, to strengthen the WTO, and to attempt to bring such policies and practices as are believed detrimental to worldwide economic efficiency to the bargaining table to achieve agreement and enforcement under the WTO.

Before delving into details, however, we should note some general points. By negotiating bilaterally, the United States is attempting to use its presumed superior bargaining power to become simultaneously the judge of another country's practices, the prosecution, the jury, and the enforcer. In many instances the trading partner may not even agree with the proposition that the practice subject to discussion is detrimental to its self-interest. Indeed, many economists would

---

27. For a review of the cigarette cases, see Lash (1992b, 16–18).

28. Indeed, Baldwin, Chen, and Nelson (1995) have produced a volume in which they analyzed U.S.-Taiwanese trade relations. The interested reader can consult that volume for a careful analysis of U.S. bilateral bargaining with a non-GATT member. Because Taiwan has not been a member of the GATT, as Baldwin, Chen, and Nelson note, it has been more subject to bilateral pressures (outside GATT rules) than other countries have been. Baldwin, Chen, and Nelson conclude that there were significantly more "third-country" effects in U.S.-Taiwanese relations because of the absence of GATT protection for third-country interests. For example, when the United States pressed Taiwan to accept more imports of American wheat, the Taiwanese were enabled to create a special category of "quality wheat" and to subject it to a lower tariff than other wheat. Since Australian wheat was "other wheat," wheat imports were diverted from Australia to the United States. The same mechanism was used to extend preference to American meat relative to that from Australia.

contend that the nation at large pays high economic costs for the agreement reached. In some cases U.S. officials are clearly responding to protectionist pressures from a given sector, and they are seen to be doing so. When they simultaneously use the rhetoric of fair trade, they appear somewhat hypocritical.

Quite aside from the availability of superior multilateral means to achieve agreement on genuinely preferable trading policies and practices, and the fact that the ensuing protection can often be downright harmful to broader American interests (if not even to the industry in question), the use of American bargaining power in bilateral negotiations risks the loss of considerable goodwill and hence makes other aspects of foreign relations more difficult. Tsurumi (1990, 2–3) asserts:

> In Japan, the image of the United States as a fat, lazy, incessant nag that blames Japan for its own problems has steadily been gaining ground. Many Japanese are fed up with Washington's endless demands. . . . With every new American demand, the United States is seen as an ever more unreasonable bully whose leadership and trust can no longer be relied upon.

Moreover, as I already pointed out, many trade problems inherently involve more than one of America's trading partners. U.S. bilateral pressure naturally focuses on products of most concern to American producers—already a source of some irritation for other countries. Those instances in which U.S. pressure has resulted in preferences given to American products have been even more difficult, however. In the case of Taiwan (where GATT rules do not govern trade), U.S. pressures have led the Taiwanese to divert trade from other sources.[29] When Taiwan sought to enter the GATT in the sum-

---

29. Baldwin, Chen, and Nelson (1995, 7) recount the drift of U.S. policy away from insistence that Taiwan abide by multilateral arrangements to more and more preferential deals for the United States. An early U.S.-Taiwan trade agreement included Taiwan's undertaking to have nondiscriminatory treatment of all trading partners. Nonetheless, the United States accepted an arrangement under which U.S. firms were given access to Taiwan's financial market but European and Japanese firms were not. The United States even negotiated a voluntary export restraint agreement under which Taiwan agreed not to export rice to any country with a per capita income above $795. Baldwin, Chen, and Nelson generalize that "the United States always set the agenda. . . . Furthermore, the bargaining process has been one-sided, with the United States proposing restrictions on Taiwan's exports or demanding market liberalizations for potential American imports, and the R.O.C. defending its protectionist position" (160).

mer of 1993, the GATT working party studying Taiwan's current trade policies "complained about restrictive market access practices and special bilateral deals with the US. It raised questions about Taiwan's allegedly discriminatory import tariff structure" (*Financial Times*, November 30, 1993, p. 6).[30]

We shall see below that third parties have protested the outcome of several bilateral negotiations with Japan and Korea, and certainly Japan and Korea have taken measures to attempt to increase exports from the United States without regard to alternative, potentially lower cost, exporters.

Bilateral Relations with Japan. There can be little doubt that trade relations with Japan have been among the most acrimonious of U.S. bilateral trade relations.[31] A large part of the acrimony has been directed toward Japan's current account balance, which has been highly positive globally and with the United States.

I showed in chapter 2 that in general current account balances are the outcome of macroeconomic variables: even if an "unfair" trader removed its "unfair" practices so that exports from its trading partners increased, in the longer run other macroeconomic adjustments would offset virtually all of that increase. Even the Clinton administration's Council of Economic Advisers (1994, 219) has acknowledged that proposition.[32]

---

30. While the GATT working party was complaining about discrimination in favor of the United States, the official U.S. position was that Taiwan should lower its tariffs unilaterally as a precondition for GATT membership.

31. There have been numerous disputes with the European Union, including the agriculture dispute that delayed the completion of the Uruguay Round. There were eleven section 301 cases filed against Japan (contrasted with twenty-six for the entire European Community) from 1975 through 1990, and Japan was named an "unfair trading country" under Super 301. Japan's bilateral trade surplus with the United States has also drawn criticism, as we shall see. It is arguable, however, that the European Community is at least as "unfair," but that its bargaining power has been greater than Japan's—hence the greater use of bilateral pressure vis-à-vis Japan. Another factor is undoubtedly that the U.S. bilateral trade balance with the European Community has been positive since 1989, while that with Japan has remained strongly negative (Council of Economic Advisers 1994, 216).

32. According to the CEA, manufactured exports from the United States to Japan might increase by $9 billion to $18 billion if all "unfair" practices were removed, while agricultural incomes of U.S. farmers would increase by an estimated 28 percent of bilateral agricultural exports if *all* Japanese agricultural export barriers were removed. (It is not stated whether this assumes that U.S. price supports and other assistance to U.S. agriculture would also be removed.) Regardless of the plausibility of the numbers, they are

Moreover, even if the total current account balance did matter, bilateral balances certainly do not. Trading nations have too much ability to substitute between different countries for any restrictions on imports or efforts to boost exports to any one country to make a significant difference. If, for example, the Japanese were constrained to export fewer cars to the United States, American imports from, and Japanese exports to, third countries would increase.

This account illustrates several phenomena: first, the extent to which trade relations with Japan have been bilateral; second, the extent to which those bilateral dealings, once started, have gained a momentum and life of their own; and third, the degree to which bilateral negotiations seem usually to have third-country or other side effects impinging both on the effectiveness of the negotiated outcome and on the multilateral system.

Historically, there had always been protectionist pressures against Japanese exports, the same as with many other countries. In the 1970s those pressures resulted in Japan's imposition of VERs on its exports of autos and steel to the United States (and Japan had earlier imposed VERs on textiles and apparel). In the early 1980s, however, the strong real appreciation of the U.S. dollar and other factors combined to increase the Japanese trade and current account balance with the United States.[33]

Rhetoric switched from exclusive attention to the effect of Japanese exports on U.S. import-competing industries to attention to Japan's domestic markets. Increasingly, allegations were heard that the Japanese protected their producers domestically in an "unfair" way, and that there were "hidden" trade barriers.

As the U.S. current account position turned more negative in the early to mid-1980s,[34] protectionist pressures increased. In response, the administration began Market-Oriented, Sector-Selective talks, in which the United States unilaterally identified specific sectors for discussions as to Japan's tariff and nontariff trade barriers. The sectors so identified were telecommunications, electronics, medical equip-

---

smaller than the Japanese bilateral current account balance with the United States.

33. The Japanese normally incur a sizable deficit on their services account with the United States.

34. The reader should recall that this sharp swing was largely a consequence of a tight monetary policy combined with loose fiscal policy following the Reagan tax cut of 1981. The dollar exchange rate, both with Japan and with major European currencies, appreciated in consequence, and large capital flows to the United States ensued (attracted largely by the high U.S. nominal and real interest rates resulting from U.S. macroeconomic policies).

73

ment and pharmaceuticals, forestry products, transportation machinery, and auto parts. The very spirit of the talks was that Japan had an obligation unilaterally to liberalize and remove trade barriers. While such actions would undoubtedly have been good for the Japanese economy (but not undertaken for political reasons probably similar to political pressures that prevent removal of protectionist measures in the United States), there was no sense in which the talks were multilateral, nor even that the United States would remove trade barriers reciprocally: the implicit threat was that failure of the MOSS talks would result in increased trade barriers against imports from Japan. As a result of those talks, Japan unilaterally reduced some trade barriers. The government undoubtedly preferred that outcome to additional protection in the United States.[35]

Subsequently, in May 1989 the United States began a Structural Impediments Initiative. That, too, was designed "to identify and solve structural problems in both countries that stand as impediments to trade and balance of payments adjustment." Macroeconomic issues such as savings levels were clearly to be the subject for bargaining. The USITC (1990, 105–6) asserted:

> A principal motivation for the SII was a mounting frustration among U.S. officials with the failure of market forces to produce a significant reduction in the United States-Japan bilateral trade deficit and other payments imbalances. . . . It was agreed that both countries had structural problems, and that those in Japan acted to impede imports while those in the United States tended to have the effect of hindering exports or reducing the competitiveness of U.S. industry.

The precedent for "talks" appears now to have been firmly set. In July 1993 the Clinton administration reached agreement with the Japanese government for "framework" talks, which are described further below. Those talks, however, carry on the tradition of bilateral bargaining with the Japanese over their economic policies and practices.

During the MOSS talks on those sector-specific aspects, another source of trade friction arose that not only illustrates the difficulties with a bilateral approach but set precedents for later intensification of bilateral dealings. The industry in question was semiconductors. Until the 1970s, the U.S. industry had been predominant. Starting in the 1970s, however, Japanese semiconductor producers had begun to gain market share. The American industry began pressuring for a variety of actions, including "improved access" to the Japanese mar-

---

35. See General Accounting Office (1988) for a detailed account.

ket.[36] The first round of industry pressure failed to achieve its objective, but when the American industry went into severe recession during 1985 and 1986, the industry resumed pressure on the U.S. administration. In the summer of 1986 the result was the semiconductor agreement with Japan.[37]

The complex, five-year agreement had several parts. I shall focus on three covenants. One part was a "secret" letter from the government of Japan to the United States that agreed that 20 percent of the Japanese market represented a reasonable "target" for American industry. Another part set a price for DRAMs below which the Japanese agreed not to sell in the U.S. market. Related to that was a third accord, under which Japan agreed to "eliminate dumping in third markets."

Although analysts disagree about some aspects of the outcome of the semiconductor agreement, there is no doubt that the Japanese raised the price at which they would sell in the U.S. market—to the detriment of American consumers of semiconductors. Worse yet, when cyclical conditions changed, a "shortage" of DRAMs raised prices and prevented U.S. computer users from filling orders in a timely fashion (USITC 1988, 4–25).

Also, the European Community protested when the United States negotiated with Japan as to minimum prices at which there would be sales in third-country markets and took the issue to the GATT. Canada joined the European Community in lodging three complaints, and a GATT panel found that the monitoring arrangements for third-country sales that Japan and the United States had agreed on were inconsistent with GATT principles.[38] Those procedures were subsequently altered in light of the GATT panel's findings.

The remaining part of the semiconductor agreement—the targeted share for U.S. firms in the Japanese market—is the most controversial. The letter in which the target was indicated has remained "secret" and not officially published. The Japanese claim that there

---

36. See Irwin (forthcoming) for a more detailed account, on which this summary is based.

37. U.S. producers had filed a section 301 case, several antidumping cases, and a number of other cases. When the semiconductor agreement was reached, they were suspended or put on hold (Low 1993, 120). In addition, the Department of Commerce announced its determination as to fair market values, which were above those at which the Japanese were selling in the U.S. market. It was made clear that sales below those prices would lead to reinstatement of antidumping suits.

38. Note that Japan was found to be violating GATT procedures.

was no formal quantitative target, but the United States in 1987 had imposed punitive duties of up to 100 percent on $300 million of Japanese imports (under procedures outlined in section 301) in retaliation for Japan's alleged failure to live up to the terms of the semiconductor agreement. The retaliation was against Japan's failure to live up to its target share ($165 million) and to monitor third-country sales as agreed on ($135 million). The United States dropped the latter charge when the GATT findings were announced, but the former remained in effect until the two countries negotiated a second semiconductor agreement in 1991. That agreement reiterated a 20 percent target (Low 1993, 123). The parties attained the 20 percent target in the final quarter of 1992, in the fourth quarter of 1993, and in the third quarter of 1994.

Quantitative indicators or targets are controversial for a variety of reasons. Most economists would argue that there is no known way for a government to "guarantee" a quantitative outcome if only market forces are at work. Supply and demand operate to determine price, and sellers and buyers voluntarily choose the quantities supplied and demanded at that price. Hence, there is no way in which the "right" share for U.S. firms in the Japanese market may be known (quite aside from the difficulty that assuring a U.S. share may be at the expense of third-country producers).

Since one of the U.S. complaints is that Japan does not permit market forces to operate, it is ironic that a U.S. government–mandated arrangement would effectively strengthen the role of bureaucrats or else encourage the formation of a cartel among foreign suppliers. How else could the Japanese attempt to assure compliance with the 20 percent quota? Clearly, either the target would occur without government commitment to it or bureaucrats and politicians would have to pressure Japanese firms to purchase from American sources. If the former, the agreement is useless (except as it sets an unfortunate precedent). If the latter, the role of government in the economy overrides market forces.[39]

---

39. For an analysis of another sector in which bureaucrats were strengthened through a VER—machine tools—see Bovard (1991b). The United States had negotiated a VER with Japan for machine tools, and certain machine tools were not elsewhere available. American companies were pressuring the Japanese authorities to make additional sales, and the Japanese were attempting to abide by the VER. Bovard quotes Bill Lane of Caterpillar as pointing out that "[t]he quotas let MITI determine which American companies would be winners and which losers" when they decided which American firms could receive the machine tools they had ordered.

The argument already carried force in the semiconductor agreement. It is now, however, far more serious as the United States has insisted on total quantitative targets for trade with Japan.[40] As stated by President Clinton's Council of Economic Advisers (1994), there have been two significant changes in the framework agreement negotiated with Japan in July 1993 from earlier MOSS and SII talks. One was that talks would be held semiannually between the U.S. president and the Japanese prime minister. The other is that the two governments would use "objective criteria" to assess progress:

> The Framework agreement states that "assessment will be based upon sets of objective criteria, either qualitative or quantitative or both as appropriate," on which the two governments will agree. In this sense the negotiation is results-oriented, with both governments agreeing that "tangible progress must be achieved." By establishing objective criteria, progress can be independently verified, allowing negotiators to agree on those areas where problems have successfully been resolved and to focus on those where progress is lacking.

The underlying reasoning for those criteria presupposes that the quantitative indicators "objectively" selected will reflect the predictable outcome of market forces. Since that cannot be the case, any indicator of targets of necessity moves from the "rules-oriented" multilateral approach of the GATT to a bilateral forum in which relative bargaining power sets the "targets."

Indeed, the Japanese refusal to accept those targets led to the breakdown of trade negotiations between Japan and the United States in February 1994, when the Japanese refused to agree to the American demand for quantitative targets and a timetable for reducing their current account surplus.

Third-party effects have appeared from many U.S. negotiations and demands in addition to those from the semiconductor agreement. For example, U.S. insistence on an increased share of the Japanese market for auto parts has led to protests from Europe and Australia, whose parts manufacturers believe that the Japan-U.S. agreement will disadvantage them (*Financial Times*, March 11, 1992,

---

40. The United States also seems more prepared to insist on quantitative targets in individual industries. In the autumn of 1993, the United States called for "prompt, substantial and sustained" increases in the sale of *U.S.* automobiles, despite the fact that the agreement for the framework talks had stipulated that any market opening should permit competition on an equal footing from all potential sources (*New York Times*, October 28, 1993, p. C1).

p. 3). The Australian Department of Foreign Affairs and Trade has stated that there is an informal arrangement between the United States and Japan whereby U.S. wheat supplies all Japanese food aid programs.[41] American pressures on the Japanese to open up their rice market are certainly suspect, as the United States subsidizes its own rice production, and Southeast Asian countries are recognized to be low-cost producers.

Furthermore, many analysts have pointed out that the United States approaches Japan bilaterally to ensure that the issues it raises are those in which America has the greatest interest. Were the United States to use the multilateral framework for dispute resolution, third country "sideswiping," trade diversion from the low-cost producer, and other side effects of American bilateral trade policies would be less destructive of the multilateral system and less of an irritant to U.S. trading partners.

In the case of Japan, it is clear that the United States has chosen to negotiate bilaterally over many issues. The use of Super 301 is yet another sad illustration of that. Before proceeding, we should consider one last instance of contravention of the GATT. In the winter of 1994, after the agreement over the Uruguay Round had been reached, the United States informed the government of Japan that it wanted reductions in the Japanese tariff on pulp and paper *in addition to those that had been negotiated during the Uruguay Round.* Not only was the U.S. announcement outside GATT bargaining, but, in effect, it reversed agreement on a deal previously concluded (*Financial Times*, March 1, 1994, p. 4).[42]

Bilateral Trade Relations with Korea. Just as the United States has held "discussions" with the Japanese over policies believed to serve

---

41. Communication from Richard Snape, July 17, 1992.

42. The United States has also revisited a number of other undertakings negotiated in the Uruguay Round. For example, in the spring of 1994 the United States and Canada were in the midst of a dispute about imports of agricultural products. The *Financial Times* (April 27, 1994, p. 7) reported: "[T]he US and Canada . . . will soon begin negotiations that could undo, at least in the short term, much of the agriculture trade liberalisation so painfully negotiated under the North American Free Trade Agreement and the General Agreement on Tariffs and Trade." The paper further reported that U.S. farm groups were urging unilateral application of U.S. legislation permitting the imposition of trade restrictions if imports threatened to have a negative impact on the U.S. farm program. But the administration was attempting to resolve the issue under Article XXVIII of the GATT—modification of schedules—despite the fact that the United States has consistently opposed European Union invocation of Article XXVIII for agricultural protection.

as barriers to U.S. exports, so too has it held talks with Korea. As a rapidly growing developing country, Korea's economic policies and structure are different in significant ways from those of Japan.[43]

First of all, Korean policy makers view their country as a poor one for which rapid economic development holds a very high priority. Korea had emerged from the aftermath of the Korean War in the 1950s as one of the poorest countries in Asia, with a high rate of inflation, multiple exchange rates, quantitative restrictions on imports, an extremely low savings and investment rate, heavy dependence on foreign aid, and all the major economic ills that plague many slowly growing developing countries.

In the 1960s Korea began policy reforms that effected a shift away from the earlier inner-oriented trade policies, much greater fiscal discipline, the elimination of inflation, and a huge structural change in the economy as savings, investment, exports, and imports all rose as shares of GDP in response to altered incentives. In the course of that transition, Korea significantly reduced import barriers,[44] although some remained. Korea made few investments in which it did not anticipate export sales, but it removed protection for the domestic market slowly.

One of the reasons for this slow progress was that the Korean authorities were facilitating heavy borrowing on the international private capital market to finance rates of investment in excess of the domestic savings rate.[45] Because the real rate of return on investment in Korea was very high, the debt so accumulated did not present a problem of the same magnitude for Korea as it did for other countries. Nevertheless, the Korean policy makers felt it important that they carefully monitor foreign borrowing and their ability to service debt. When the Korean savings rate had reached 35 percent in the mid-

---

43. There are considerable similarities between the sorts of trade disputes and issues the United States has had with Korea and those it has had with Taiwan, although Taiwan has had less protection because it is not a member of the GATT. But pressures to open markets, restrict imports, enter into voluntary export restraint agreements, adopt more restrictive intellectual property rights legislation, and otherwise reduce the current account deficit have been similar.

44. See Frank, Kim, and Westphal (1975) for an account of the Korean trade and payments regime in the 1950s and the changes that took place during the early years of reform.

45. Korea had ceased receiving foreign aid in the 1960s and shifted to the private international capital market. For a fuller account of Korean-U.S. international economic relations, including the aid-receiving period, see Krueger (1993a, chap. 8).

1980s, the Korean current account swung into surplus for the first time, and the authorities began repaying debt. Korean outstanding debt fell from its peak of $47.1 million in 1985 to $39.8 million in 1987 and to $34.0 million in 1990 (World Bank, 1993, Korea country table). The level of foreign debt had been unpopular with the Korean public. Efforts to reduce debt were made partly in response to popular demands as the country was shifting toward more representative and democratic political institutions—a shift the United States strongly endorsed.

The Korean current account surpluses became a target of U.S. bilateral talks with the Koreans, however. The United States had pressured the Koreans to purchase more U.S. imports and to let the currency appreciate to facilitate that practice.[46] The USITC (1988) reported, "Since registering a $7.4 billion trade surplus with the U.S. in 1986, Korea has been under increasing pressure from the U.S. government to revalue the won at a more rapid rate than has occurred thus far." The USITC further noted that "currency revaluation [was] one of the most contentious issues between the two countries in 1987." Since American focus was on the bilateral trade balance,[47] and Korea was incurring a large trade deficit with Japan,[48] one part of the response of the Korean authorities was to undertake a "trade diversification" program. Under that program, the Korean govern-

---

46. Note that, from the viewpoint of economic efficiency, removal of remaining Korean tariff protection should have preceded currency appreciation. The fact that the U.S. authorities pressed for *both* import barrier removal and currency appreciation suggests that the United States was seeking to reduce Korean exports to the U.S. market as well as to induce more U.S. exports to Korea.

47. When the United States was considering extending free trade arrangements to other countries in the late 1980s, the Institute for International Economics invited papers by authors from a number of potential partner countries. The paper focusing on a possible Korean-U.S. free trade agreement noted, "What worries many in Korea is that the United States may view a bilateral free trade agreement as a remedy for its external imbalance" (Park and Yoo 1989, 157).

48. The Korean government provided an interesting explanation: "If the Korean won is considered undervalued against the dollar, creating a trade surplus with the U.S., logic would dictate that the won must be considered overvalued against the Japanese yen, creating Korea's trade deficit with Japan. Korea's dilemma lies in the fact that because the Korean won is not a major currency in international financial markets, it cannot be devalued against the yen while it is revalued simultaneously against the dollar." (Republic of Korea 1989, 48). One must wonder how even a major currency would achieve that objective!

ment announced plans to "freeze its trade surplus with the United States and encourage its exporters to seek markets elsewhere." Importers also needed special approval for imports from countries with which Korea was incurring a bilateral trade deficit (USITC 1989, 127). The Korean government targeted 365 products traditionally imported from Japan for diversification and provided the U.S. government with a list of names and addresses of Korean end-users.[49] It also set import regulations regarding beef to encourage importation of United States beef in preference to range-fed beef (Republic of Korea 1989, 47), deliberately opened agricultural and industrial markets in which the United States had an interest first (Republic of Korea 1989, 17), sent buying missions to the United States,[50] and provided special credits to finance American exports to Korea (Republic of Korea 1989, 51).

Korea has also been a major target of antidumping, countervailing duty, and unfair trade (section 301) actions. From 1975 to 1990, the United States brought eight section 301 cases against Korea, of which seven were resolved with market-opening actions. Low (1993, 91) notes:

[There has been] a far higher success rate scored with Japan and Korea than with any other countries. . . . The United States appears, therefore, to have been much more successful in persuading Japan and Korea to do what they asked than the European Community. How much longer the retaliation threat can be expected to work on Japan and Korea is a matter of speculation.

Korea has also entered into VERs covering a variety of goods, including textiles and apparel. During the Gulf War, Korea (like Hong Kong) was pressured to accept a lower export quota to the United States as part of its "war contribution" as the United States increased Turkey's quota (Low 1993, 122).

While undertaking those actions, the United States was also negotiating with Korea over treatment of a number of commodities and markets. We need not delve into the arrangements in all markets. In 1988, a fairly typical year, the United States negotiated imports of wine, beef, and cigarettes, in addition to pressuring for appreciation

---

49. See Republic of Korea (1989), especially page 5, for a fuller account.

50. The explanation given was as follows: "Normally, the seller travels to meet the buyer. However, since potential American exporters to Korea have a geographic disadvantage in comparison to [sic] their Japanese counterparts, Korea has taken the initiative by sending frequent buying missions to all regions of the United States" (Republic of Korea 1989, 52).

of the exchange rate and tariff reduction.[51] The treatment of beef, in particular, drew protests from Australia, a third-country exporter.

The United States also protested Korea's protection of the domestic insurance market. Finally, under pressure, the Korean authorities did permit two foreign companies to enter the Korean insurance market. Not surprisingly, both of them were American (Cho 1988).

America's most blatant bilateral market opening in Korea was in intellectual property rights, however. The USTR placed Korea on the priority watch list under Special 301. Under pressure from the United States, Korea strengthened its intellectual property law and enforcement, starting in 1987. For U.S. firms, though, the law was made retroactive to 1980 for books and 1982 for software. Protests from the European Community and Japan ensued, and the European Community suspended Korea's eligibility for preferential tariff treatment under the Generalized System of Preferences (Young 1989, 39). The USTR, however, characterized the Korean changes in intellectual property rights as a "dramatic" improvement (USITC 1990, 148).

Koreans have deeply resented U.S. pressure for market opening and exchange rate appreciation. While the United States certainly achieved some short-term goals, it must be questioned whether the long-term results of U.S. pressure will be a more open Korean market, or instead a more slowly growing Korean economy with more political resistance to trade liberalization than would have occurred through a multilateral, albeit possibly slower, liberalization process. As with Japan, third-country effects are clearly important. Over the longer term, multilateral approaches can more effectively meet the legitimate underlying U.S. concerns, with less political backlash in Korea and fewer complications in trading relations with other countries. Overriding all of those issues, of course, is the proposition that U.S. foreign policy concerns in Korea go considerably beyond trade issues. To have had such trade friction visibly at the center of U.S.-Korean relations has certainly been detrimental to the larger relationship.

Conclusions

There can be little doubt that the United States has shifted increasingly to bilateral negotiations with individual trading partners, has

---

51. It has been pointed out that tariff reduction may follow most-favored-nation rules (although the "import diversification" was clearly not a most-favored-nation program), but that when reductions are in response to U.S. pressures, tariffs are more likely to be reduced on goods of greater interest to the United States.

placed increasing pressure on its partners to open their markets in ways that benefit U.S. producers, and has restrained exports when U.S. import-competing interests are politically potent. While a commitment to the multilateral system remains, an increasing number of bilateral actions raise questions as to the degree of that commitment.

Simultaneously, despite American rhetoric about the openness and lack of trade barriers to entry into the U.S. market, examination of even a few VERs, the use of Super 301, and some aspects of bilateral trade relations with Japan and Korea strongly indicates that U.S. policies and practices are not beyond reproach when judged by standards of American rhetoric.

The increasing attention to bilateral trade negotiations must inevitably raise questions in the minds of the rest of the world as to the degree of commitment by the United States to the preservation and strengthening of the multilateral system. Before turning to that issue and to ways in which the United States could alter its policies to improve the functioning of the multilateral system, we should focus on yet another aspect of bilateral American policies: regional trading arrangements. They are the subject of chapter 5.

5

The North American Free Trade Agreement, the Western Hemisphere Free Trade Agreement, and the Multilateral Trading System

The schizophrenia between multilateralism and bilateralism in trade policy is most evident in U.S. bilateral negotiations over trade issues with the European Community, Japan, Korea, and other countries. An additional question for U.S. trade policy and for the global trading system, however, is how the North American Free Trade Agreement and proposals to enlarge it into a Western Hemisphere free trade agreement relate to the multilateral system.

Because any free trade agreement provides for preferential tariff treatment among countries, a free trade agreement is inherently a departure from the basic most-favored-nation principle of the GATT and the WTO. But some preferential trading arrangements are consistent with GATT principles, and the important question is how such arrangements are related to the multilateral system.

That question is the focus of this chapter. I shall argue that the European Union, at least during its first quarter-century, was consistent with the open multilateral system because external trade liberalization was proceeding apace with the internal removal of trade barriers, except for agriculture. NAFTA, and any successor Western

Hemisphere free trade agreement, can also evolve in a way that strengthens the open multilateral system. There is, however, a danger that NAFTA and its successor might emerge in a manner that further weakens multilateralism.

To set forth the argument, I first provide background information on the GATT and WTO provisions with respect to preferential trading arrangements, their relative importance in the past forty years, the U.S.-Canada Free Trade Agreement, NAFTA, and the proposed Western Hemisphere free trade agreement. Then I consider some of the questions that arise about the effect of NAFTA and a possible Western Hemisphere free trade agreement on the open multilateral system.

Background

The GATT principles as formulated permitted preferential trading arrangements[1] under certain conditions.[2] Such trading arrangements had to be uniform and across-the-board (and not relate only to a few sectors of the economy). In addition, they were not to reduce member countries' trade with the rest of the world.[3]

International trade lawyers generally agree that the GATT provi-

---

1. A considerable economics literature exists on preferential trading arrangements and their effects. Economists distinguish three types of arrangements: a free trade agreement, under which members have no trade barriers to imports from other members, but retain their separate external tariffs; a customs union, under which members have no trade barriers with each other and a common external tariff; and a common market, which is a customs union in which movements of labor and capital between member countries are unrestricted.

2. In the economics literature, analysis of preferential arrangements has largely centered on customs unions. Their effect on global economic efficiency is ambiguous, because lowering of tariffs among members can either "create" trade by increasing imports of items previously domestically produced at higher cost or "divert" trade by having goods previously imported from third countries (at low cost) now produced in member countries behind the joint tariff wall. To be sure, we must consider other effects, such as lowered consumer prices, to make a comprehensive judgment. The larger trade diversion is, however, the greater the likelihood that the customs union will reduce the potential gains from trade. For a survey of the literature, see Corden (1984).

3. Indeed, if joining a preferential trading arrangement was shown to damage a third nonmember country's export markets, the country joining the preferential arrangement was obligated under GATT rules to provide compensation to the nonmember. See Dam (1970) for an elaboration of those and other aspects of GATT provisions regarding preferential arrangements.

85

sions regarding preferential trading arrangements (Article XXIV) are somewhat vague. That reflects in part the fact that few contemplated the emergence of regional arrangements as a significant factor in the international economy when they considered the future of the international economy after World War II. The United States, which wanted to make all preferential trading arrangements illegal, and the United Kingdom, which wanted to preserve Commonwealth preferences, agreed to the article.

Indeed, with the exception of the European Community, for the most part regional trading arrangements became less important. Commonwealth preferences diminished in importance and were finally abandoned, and arrangements such as the European Payments Union gave way to multilateral payment arrangements as soon as the European economies resumed their economic growth. Even when developing countries, which by and large distrusted the international economic system and failed to participate fully, did form preferential trading arrangements (as in the Latin American Free Trade Agreement, the Central American Common Market, the East African Common Market, and the Association of Southeast Asian Nations), they were largely unimportant for participating countries relative to their trade with the rest of the world. Most such arrangements either stagnated or, as with the East African Common Market and the Latin American Free Trade Agreement, were disbanded. The Association of Southeast Asian Nations, the most enduring and successful of the developing countries' preferential trading arrangements to date, has been avowedly outer-oriented, and until recent years, preferences among the ASEAN countries were very small.

The one highly visible exception to the diminishing importance of preferential arrangements was the European Community. After the Treaty of Rome (when a number of skeptics doubted that the European Common Market would hold together), the increased trade among the original six, the accession of Britain, Spain, Portugal, Greece, Denmark, and Ireland, and other moves toward European integration surprised most observers. Given the high rates of growth of the EC countries and the liberalization of the world economy,[4] however, EC integration increased EC trade with the rest of the world as well as within the European Community.

In consequence, other countries viewed the European example benignly. And, given the European Union's low and falling trade

---

4. Several significant GATT rounds of multilateral tariff negotiations coincided with the major steps in EC integration, partly as a result of deliberate U.S. policy.

barriers to manufacturers as well as the rapid expansion of its trade with nonmember countries, many observers attributed the rapid growth of trade to the formation of the Common Market. In addition, it was widely recognized that there were unique political motives behind European integration, which evidently served to keep it on track when difficulties and roadblocks to further integration arose.

Even so, until the early 1980s, virtually all trends in the international economy were toward greater global integration. Preferential arrangements appeared to be adjuncts to the multilateral system or failures.[5] Then, in the early 1980s, the USTR announced his intention of following a "two-track" approach: the United States would support agreements for further trade liberalization through the GATT but would enter into preferential trading arrangements with countries that wanted to go beyond the GATT in integrating their economies.

The idea was born, at least in part, out of frustration with the procedure for launching a new round of trade negotiations under the GATT. When the 1982 ministerial meeting in Geneva ended without any agreement to proceed further with trade liberalization after the Tokyo Round, then-USTR William Brock announced that the United States would attempt to achieve further trade liberalization in a "GATT plus" with "like-minded" trading partners. The essential idea was that, if further trade liberalization through the GATT would be blocked, those countries that were willing to proceed could do so through preferential arrangements. The economic success of those free-trading nations would then induce other countries to join in the "GATT-plus" arrangements and would ultimately make it too costly for countries to abstain. In that way, it was thought, further progress could be achieved even in the absence of another round of GATT-sponsored multilateral trade negotiations.

Initially, little seemed to happen, as the signing of a U.S.-Israel free trade agreement was the first and only immediate consequence. Moreover, by 1986, agreement had been reached on another round, and the Uruguay Round of trade negotiations was launched in Punta del Este. In addition, the Uruguay Round contained a commitment to start liberalizing trade in agriculture and was the first round in which the developing countries took an active role. Attention then moved back to the multilateral system.

---

5. The European Community was regarded as a great success. The European Free Trade Area, which consisted of those industrialized European countries not in the European Community (including the United Kingdom, until it left to join), was viewed as an arrangement of secondary importance even to its members contrasted with their links to other countries.

In the mid-1980s, however, Canada and the United States agreed to trade talks to enter into a free trade agreement. After protracted negotiations, the two countries agreed to establish the U.S.-Canada Free Trade Agreement. The Canadian parliament and the U.S. Congress approved the agreement, which was signed on January 2, 1988, and commenced on January 1, 1989.

The economies of the two countries as well as the legal systems were similar in a number of regards. The United States and Canada were already large trading partners; Canada exported largely primary commodities to the United States in exchange for manufactures. Even so, the schedule for arriving at a full-blown free trade agreement was relatively drawn out: the parties scheduled tariff reductions over a nine-year period. On January 1, 1998, there will be no tariffs.

Initially, the prospective U.S.-Canada Free Trade Agreement was regarded as a natural linkage between two neighboring economies.[6] The United States had continued its support of the multilateral system. The U.S.-Israel free trade agreement appeared to cover such a small percentage of U.S. trade and to have such an obvious political basis as to be *sui generis*. The U.S.-Canada pact seemed unremarkable as it simply strengthened trading ties between two "natural" trading partners[7] to the advantage of both.[8]

Perceptions and realities changed sharply, however, when the Mexican president, Carlos Salinas de Gortari, announced that Mexico would also seek to negotiate a free trade agreement with the United

---

6. That is not to say that there were not political objections to the pact. There were a number of contentious items during the negotiations, and opposition to the agreement has been an issue in Canadian elections.

7. Krugman (1991b) argued that even the Mexican accession to the free trade agreement was "natural."

8. There were two other preferential trading arrangements in which the United States participated. The first was the Generalized System of Preferences. Developing countries had for years sought preferential treatment of their imports in developed countries' markets. The industrialized countries had agreed on a Generalized System of Preferences under which tariff reductions and exemptions were granted to developing countries on a specified range of commodities they exported to the industrialized countries. Imports from developing countries are still granted tariff preferences on a number of items.

The second departure from nondiscriminatory trade was the Caribbean Basin Initiative, under which the United States unilaterally extended preferential (usually zero-tariff) treatment to imports from eligible Caribbean countries. See Krueger (1993a, chap. 7) for particulars.

States.[9] That reversal of long-standing Mexican policies caught officials in other countries by surprise. The Mexican motives were several. Perhaps most important, Mexico had already greatly liberalized its trade regime[10] and had undertaken a number of other policy reforms. Accession to a free trade agreement would signal Mexico's commitment to maintain the new economic policies and thus would lend credibility to the reforms. Another major consideration was the belief that a free trade agreement would attract much larger private foreign capital flows to Mexico.[11]

For a variety of reasons, the Bush administration was receptive to the approach. Because the Mexican government had undertaken politically difficult but necessary economic reforms, the administration deemed it essential to demonstrate American support for those reforms. Thus, for foreign policy reasons alone, support was forthcoming. In addition, however, the Mexican announcement was consistent with the administration's "two-track" approach to trade policy and its announced willingness to enter into preferential arrangements with "like-minded" countries.

With that commitment, negotiations started for a free trade agreement. There was, however, an immediate question: how would Mexican entry affect the already negotiated U.S.-Canada Free Trade Agreement? The issues were several and complex. At first it appeared that the United States and Mexico would negotiate a separate agreement. That raised questions about differences in the U.S. treatment of Canada and Mexico, about differences in legal rulings that might arise,[12] and about the "loss" to Canada of the value of concessions won in the earlier negotiation. Analysts pointed out that the Canadians had conceded to the United States in some regards to gain preferential treatment in the American market for some of their products. If Mexico were accorded similar treatment for commodities that were competitive with the Canadian ones in question, that would reduce

---

9. The Mexican Senate approved that in May 1990. For particulars, see Auerbach (1990).

10. As part of its reforms, Mexico finally joined the GATT in 1987.

11. There was concern at the time that the East European countries would attract attention and resources away from Mexico and other developing countries.

12. One of the achievements of the U.S.-Canada Free Trade Agreement was to establish a binational panel for dispute settlement. There were legitimate concerns that a separate panel for Mexico might even lead to differences in rulings and conflicts in trade law. See Schott (1989) and the papers contained therein for a discussion.

the value of the concessions Canada obtained. Analysts pointed to further potential difficulties of that sort if and when still other countries negotiated to join the free trade agreement.

There were additional concerns. One focused on the possibility of a "hub-spoke" system, under which the United States would negotiate free trade agreements with many Latin American countries individually. Under that scenario the United States would have preferential access to all the other markets, while each trading partner would have access only to the admittedly large one. That would have given the United States an advantage over other countries that had entered free trade agreements when imported components from, for example, Canada entered the U.S. market duty-free while Mexican producers of the same commodity paid the tariff-ridden price.[13]

A final concern focused on the possibility that if countries acceded to the free trade agreement sequentially, there could be successive rounds of trade diversion. If, for example, Mexico's exports of men's shirts to the United States increased after the signing of a free trade agreement because of the tariff preference, Mexico might lose that market to a country such as Colombia, were that country to join at a later date.[14] The sequence could, at least in theory, be repeated several times, as other countries joined, if each had lower costs than the preceding entrant. While it would be a coincidence if each new entrant had costs lower than the preceding entrant by just enough to compete once the margin of preference was extended to it, the potential for uneconomic investment because of future trade diversion nonetheless remained.

After discussing those issues, Canada, Mexico, and the United States finally decided to enter into three-way negotiations to formulate NAFTA. Shortly thereafter, the U.S. administration recognized the dangers of exclusivity and announced the "Enterprise for the Americas," under which the United States declared that it was willing to negotiate with other Latin American countries for entry into a Western Hemisphere free trade agreement. The Chileans, who al-

---

13. Of course, any country concerned about that possibility could have prevented it by lowering its tariffs to zero.

14. The concern over potential future problems had an immediate application. In 1983 the Reagan administration had extended tariff preferences to the Caribbean countries under the Caribbean Basin Initiative, as already mentioned. The prospect of Mexico's entering NAFTA eroded the value of Caribbean Basin Initiative preferences, and there were reports of the relocation of plants from CBI-eligible countries to Mexico in anticipation of the free trade agreement. See Krueger (1993a) for a discussion.

ready had a liberal trade regime, indicated their eagerness to do so and have been officially informed by the USTR that they are eligible to negotiate.[15]

Several features of NAFTA should be noted. We have seen that Article XXIV of the GATT endorses across-the-board preferential arrangements or interim arrangements to that end. Negotiations for NAFTA proceeded to a considerable degree sector by sector, however.[16] Thus, separate arrangements were made for textiles and apparel, for automobiles and parts, for maritime shipping, and for a variety of other sectors. For agriculture, there were essentially three bilateral agreements, with much in common. The entire agreement is about 2,000 pages long, prompting some to wonder why it requires so much to say that there will be no trade barriers!

Finally, there were sectors that remained outside the free trade agreement because of protectionist pressures in member countries. For the United States, pressures for protection kept coastal shipping outside the agreement, while Mexico exempted its petroleum deposits. Moreover, restrictions on flows of unskilled workers to the United States were not relaxed.

Once NAFTA was made public, political opposition mounted in the United States, and concerns intensified. Many opposed the agreement until environmental and labor codes were negotiated. Such side agreements, taken to extremes, could wipe out or substantially reduce the potential gains from the agreement. Mexico, after all, is relatively abundant in unskilled labor and should find its comparative advantage vis-à-vis the United States, at least in the short run, in low-productivity, labor-intensive industries. If those industries are subject to wage restrictions that eliminate or severely reduce their cost advantage, they will be unable to export to the U.S. market.[17]

---

15. The Clinton administration announced its intention to expand to a Western Hemisphere free trade agreement in December 1994, and negotiations for Chile's accession were set to begin in 1995.

16. The sectoral approach had several dimensions. First, the pace at which trade barriers were to be reduced differed for different sectors. Second, the parties negotiated "rules of origin" for individual sectors. Third, the parties negotiated special rules governing access in a number of areas such as financial services and phytosanitary regulations. See Hufbauer and Schott (1992) for an analysis.

17. Mexican wages are lower than U.S. wages largely because the productivity of labor is lower in Mexico. When wages are artificially constrained to be higher, the effect is to increase the labor costs per unit of output and, given the productivity differential, to reduce or eliminate the competitive

The same concerns surround the environmental issues. In all industrialized countries, considerable environmental damage accompanied economic growth. It has only been as living standards have increased (and perhaps as the environment has deteriorated) that countries have developed a willingness to accept some of the costs of cleanup.[18]

After NAFTA had been negotiated in the summer of 1993, the Clinton administration negotiated "side agreements" with Mexico on three issues: labor, the environment, and actions that might be taken in the event of "import surges." Three commissions have been established to investigate complaints that may be brought about each of those issues.[19]

Are NAFTA and the Prospective Western Hemisphere Free Trade Agreement Compatible with the Open Multilateral System?

There is no doubt that tariffs and other barriers to trade among the three North American countries will be reduced over the course of the transition period. Indeed, trade barriers have already fallen considerably with respect to U.S.-Canada trade.[20]

---

advantage Mexican firms might otherwise have. Hufbauer and Schott (1993, 173) report that the wage differential for hourly production workers between the United States and Mexico was 8.0 while the productivity differential, as measured by value added per worker, was 8.2. This could be interpreted to suggest that American labor was relatively cheaper than Mexican labor, as unit labor costs are lower.

18. It has been estimated that a per capita income of around $5,000 is the turning point for environmental concerns. That is, when people are very poor, they are too concerned with day-to-day survival to be able to devote time or resources to environmental protection. When per capita incomes reach $5,000, countries have historically begun devoting more resources to environmental cleanup. It may well be that other factors (such as the shift to more service jobs) account for part of this observed change. But there are a number of reasons to believe that Mexicans are already concerned about their environment. Moreover, with more rapid economic growth, Mexican per capita income will reach the $5,000 range sooner than otherwise. By speeding economic growth and enabling the attainment of that level sooner, NAFTA may be the best possible approach to cleaning up the environment. See Grossman and Alan Krueger (1992) for an analysis of environmental spending as a function of per capita income.

19. See Hufbauer and Schott (1993, 157–65) for a description of those provisions and arrangements.

20. That is not to say that all is proceeding smoothly. At the time of writing, Canada and the United States are engaged in a serious trade dispute

There is no reason why NAFTA needs to be inconsistent with the open multilateral trading system and with the ideals of free trade discussed in chapter 2. All GATT obligations would be recognized, and the contracting parties would in effect pursue "deeper integration" and encourage others to join them on the same terms, while maintaining low or zero protection against imports from countries outside the preferential area. The free trade agreement would then be an association of like-minded free trading nations that desired to go beyond GATT obligations and remove nonborder, as well as border, impediments to trade.[21]

It is not guaranteed, however, that NAFTA will evolve into a Western Hemisphere free trade agreement in such a "GATT-plus" manner. Given the American propensity for bilateralism seen in chapter 4, there are some legitimate concerns that a Western Hemisphere free trade agreement will become a GATT substitute, either by intention or by evolution.

Economists concerned with the functioning of the multilateral system and observers in East Asia and in Europe have several bases for concern. First, some fear that the free trade agreement is really a way of "exporting" American administered protection to third countries and that it will divert rather than create trade. Second, some contend that the free trade agreement is, either by design or effect, drawing American attentions and support away from the multilateral system. Third, some believe that in basing the free trade agreement on regional considerations and limiting accession of other countries, signatories will have little or no intent for a "GATT-plus" arrangement to eventuate. The fourth concern centers on the question of additional entrants. If countries negotiate free trade agreements separately with each new entrant, there are enormous possibilities for legal discrepancies between rules between different pairs of countries. If, for example, the United States negotiates with Chile for a free trade agreement, how can provisions differ from those of NAFTA? If

---

over Canadian wheat exports to the United States (*New York Times*, April 22, 1994, p. C1). Canada was threatening retaliation by imposing tariffs on U.S. exports of wine and bourbon to Canada. Moreover, the bilateral dispute settlement panel settled a timber dispute in Canada's favor: the United States removed its duties on Canadian imports of softwood lumber, but instead of refunding duties already paid, announced that it was "in process of evaluating what our future course would be" (*Financial Times*, August 24, 1994, p. 4).

21. The European Community's 1992 commitments appear to have been largely of that kind. Although there was concern that the 1992 integration might result in "Fortress Europe," most commitments between EC members turned out to be liberalizing.

they do differ, will NAFTA provisions be altered or will the NAFTA partners then be subject to trading arrangements with the United States that differ from those with Chile? In the case of agriculture, where there are separate bilateral agreements, it is difficult to imagine how there could be a fourth entrant. Even for other provisions, the mechanics of negotiation (whether to reopen the existing agreements, how to accommodate the concerns of yet another member without renegotiating issues settled among the three) raise serious questions.

I shall first address those concerns and then consider why we should view a drift toward regional trading blocs with alarm.

Is NAFTA a Way of Exporting U.S. Protection? Chapters 3 and 4 analyzed concerns over the U.S. drift toward administered protection. If there were no drift toward regionalism, the propensity to use administered protection in the manner it is used in the United States would in any event be a cause for concern.[22] As noted in chapter 3, one of the major Canadian motives in seeking a free trade agreement with the United States was to reduce the risks of antidumping and countervailing duty suits in Canadian-American trade (Rugman and Anderson 1987).

With the inauguration of NAFTA, however, fears have intensified among U.S. trading partners. This is so since it is possible, if not probable, that U.S. antidumping and countervailing duty measures might be used against third-country exporters in the event that NAFTA members substantially increase their exports of goods to the United States.

Suppose, for example, that Mexican exports of instruments (which are currently imported largely from East Asian countries) increase greatly under NAFTA. One possible response of U.S. import-competing producers would be to file antidumping cases against East Asian exporters. If they won those cases, the increase in U.S. imports from Mexico could be partially or entirely offset by the reduced exports from East Asian countries. That would represent a clear-cut case of trade diversion that resulted from the administration of U.S. trade laws, rather than from the underlying economics of the agreement.[23]

---

22. It seems clear that the best resolution to the question of how to meet legitimate concerns about injury in the event of dumping lies along the lines of an international agreement on competition policy, under which countries would treat domestic and foreign firms equally and make them subject to the same tests of conduct.

23. Even Canadian or Mexican producers are not exempt from antidumping and countervailing duty actions. The U.S.-Canada Free Trade Agreement

In addition to issues surrounding administered protection, the agreement itself raises concerns about another way in which the United States may export protection. That is, the rules of origin contained in the agreement may export American protection to Mexican and Canadian markets. Some 200 pages are devoted to "rules of origin." Those are necessary in a free trade agreement (when each country has its own tariff rates) to determine when preferential tariff treatment will apply and when it will not for commodities, part of which are produced in the free trade agreement member and part of which are produced abroad. Rules of origin can be, and in some sectors in NAFTA are, protective devices. Thus, in NAFTA, for textiles and apparel to qualify for preferential treatment and lowered duties, they must pass a "triple transformation test" under which the final product must be made from materials made in NAFTA countries, which in turn must have been fabricated from fibers grown or produced in North America (Hufbauer and Schott 1993, 44). Thus, garments made in Mexico with textile fabrics imported from Japan would not qualify for preferential tariffs.

Rules of origin for automobiles were also devised with a view to protecting U.S. auto producers, who were described as "elated" with the agreement. While there must be rules of origin (or else anything imported into the free trade agreement member that had tariffs higher than transport costs between members would be imported through the low-tariff country), countries can use those rules to "export" protection. This seems to have been the effect of some rules of origin under NAFTA.[24]

The problems with rules of origin were already well illustrated under the U.S.-Canada agreement in the Honda dispute between Canada and the United States. In that case the Canadian exporter

---

has been in effect since 1988, and there have already been a number of disputes. They have centered on such items as beer, cars, lumber, and men's suits (*New York Times*, February 18, 1992, pp. 1, C6). One of the most acrimonious of those, Honda cars, was based on the interpretation of rules of origin, which are discussed below.

Administered protection has proceeded so far in the United States that at least two prominent American senators, Robert Dole and Max Baucus, have urged the Mexicans to bring a countervailing duty case against Canadian wheat. They asserted that bringing a countervailing duty case "would indicate a strong desire [on the part of the Mexicans] to guarantee that the NAFTA will provide continent-wide trade, free of export subsidies." Note the absence of any mention of American subsidies to wheat producers (*Financial Times*, July 21, 1993, p. 3).

24. See Krueger (1993a) for a fuller discussion of that issue.

had imported parts, some from the United States and some from Japan, for assembly into the Honda automobiles that were in turn to be exported to the United States. Believing that parts made in the United States were "100 percent" NAFTA, the producers thought that their product met the rule of origin standard (Ritchie 1992). But the American position was that only the American-made portion of the parts could count toward meeting the rule of origin test—50 percent of the value of parts used had to originate within the NAFTA member. The deputy chief Canadian negotiator of the American-Canadian agreement and former ambassador to the United States asserted:

> Recent American trade actions . . . have raised doubts about America's willingness to honor its commitments and have provoked a rising tide of criticism from Canadian government, industry and labor leaders. The strongest criticism has come from those who most strongly supported the FTA. Today only one Canadian in four believes the Free Trade Agreement has worked. . . . If the U.S. is unwilling to play by the rules established under the agreement, even this limited support is likely to evaporate.[25]

Initial reports of Mexico's experience during the first half-year of NAFTA indicated increased paperwork and confusion as a result of rules of origin (*New York Times*, June 21, 1994, p. A1). Some firms even claimed that the tariffs confronting their products on entry into the United States had increased (*New York Times*, June 21, 1994, p. C2).[26]

Diversion of Attention from the Multilateral System. Given limited resources in the office of the USTR and in other federal agencies responsible for formulating and implementing trade policy, it was inevitable that NAFTA would result in some diversion of attention from the multilateral system. If only because many senior USTR officials were involved in dealing with representatives of Canada, Mexico, and various industry and labor groups in negotiating the

---

25. The account given above is grossly simplified to make it comprehensible. The problems with rules of origin arise because of ambiguities as to what percentage of a product "originates" in the country producing it. NAFTA raises the 50 percent level for autos under the U.S.-Canada Free Trade Agreement to 62.5 percent, but the basis for calculating the percentage North American is also changed.

26. The firm quoted is Mattel, a producer of toys that had previously been imported duty-free into the United States and that faced a 6.8 to 12 percent duty after NAFTA came into effect.

agreement, there was simply less time for those same people to address the Uruguay Round and other problems of the multilateral system.

There can thus be little question that NAFTA shifted the focus—at least to some extent—of American officials. Ironically, analysts initially assumed that NAFTA would have relatively little political opposition, while the Uruguay Round agreement would encounter much more.

In fact, the opposition to NAFTA reversed those forecasts. Nonetheless, senior politicians, confronted with the necessity of defending and pushing NAFTA, are diverted, at least to a degree, from the multilateral framework and talks. Indeed, addressing the issue of which Latin American countries will be eligible for entry into a Western Hemisphere free trade agreement must constitute a focal point of activity in the office of the USTR as the date for announcement of the eligible list approaches.

U.S. officials have been adamant that their negotiation of the U.S.-Canada Free Trade Agreement and NAFTA did not detract from their efforts in the Uruguay Round. There are two reasons why we may question that insistence, however. First, the very fact of NAFTA negotiations led Europeans and others to wonder how committed the United States was to the Uruguay Round and to the GATT system itself. Second, the prospects for NAFTA have, at times, led politicians to make pronouncements that sound dangerously as if they believe that a regional trading arrangement can substitute for the multilateral system. To the extent that such a belief, whether articulated or not, reduced the amount of attention and energy the American administration devoted to completing the Uruguay Round (and then strengthening the WTO), or enabled congressmen to vote for measures that undermine the international trading system in the belief that regional trade can substitute, NAFTA exacted a significant cost for the multilateral system.

How important that diversion of attention has been is difficult to judge. Whether it was a factor in the Clinton administration's difficulty in setting trade policy during its first year in office is an open question.

Rules of Accession. If NAFTA is truly a "GATT-plus" arrangement, it should be open to all other countries to enter. Instead, NAFTA is touted as a regional arrangement, and the accession clause is very vague: "Any country or group of countries may accede to this Agreement subject to such terms and conditions as may be agreed between such country or countries and the Commission and following approval in accordance with the applicable legal procedures in each country" (Article 2205(1)).

According to the *Financial Times* (March 24, 1994, p. 4), many Western Hemisphere countries are pressing for entry. The Clinton administration has already indicated its willingness to negotiate next with Chile over membership. But the accession clause permits each country already in NAFTA to veto the entry of a newcomer.[27] Thus, Australia or Taiwan could undertake to have completely free trade with the United States, adhere to all provisions of NAFTA, and yet be denied entry. Without elucidating criteria for accession of other countries, the NAFTA treaty itself appears suspect. Moreover, as noted earlier, Canada and Mexico each bargained with the United States to gain preferences for themselves. Neither of those countries is likely to welcome a new entrant with open arms if that entrant exports commodities to the United States that are closely competitive with its own U.S. exports.

The behavior of the leaders of the countries involved in the Caribbean Basin Initiative proves that this issue is not academic.[28] Those countries were unilaterally granted preferential access to the U.S. market in the 1980s. When NAFTA was proposed, leaders of the Caribbean Basin Initiative countries protested vehemently about the losses they were incurring as Mexico became a more attractive location once it, too, was eligible for shipping goods duty-free to the United States. It is hard to believe that Mexico and Canada will not react similarly if, for example, Brazil and Australia are negotiating for membership.

Would a World Divided into Trading Blocs Be Undesirable? In addition to the immediate concerns enumerated above, a broader issue arises in connection with regional trading arrangements, especially when accession clauses, sectoral arrangements, and other features appear to be inconsistent with GATT principles. That is, there is a potential danger that the movement toward regionalism could set in motion a series of events that ultimately lead to the division of the world into trading blocs, with weaker trading ties between blocs and more trade within blocs than under the current multilateral system.

One basis for concern is that the formation of NAFTA, along

---

27. There is also a "nonapplication" provision, so that a country could be denied NAFTA benefits without being denied entry (Hufbauer and Schott 1993, 114).

28. See Krueger (1993a, chap. 6) for a description of the Caribbean Basin Initiative.

with the continuing EC arrangements, might prompt East and Southeast Asian countries (perhaps including Australia and New Zealand) to form their own trading bloc.[29] That might then leave the world with three large trading blocs and a few regions largely left out of the world trading system.[30]

Some observers have responded by suggesting that a world of several large trading blocs might not be so bad. Krugman (1991a) has even developed a model to assess the effects of dividing the world into such blocs, although he found three to be the worst number from the vantage point of world welfare. Krugman also assumed, however, that each bloc imposed tariffs that were "optimal" from that bloc's viewpoint, where optimality was determined by the degree of monopoly power in trade, which is not in fact how trade is implemented.

Given existing protectionist pressures in North America and Europe, the emergence of regional trading blocs would almost surely lead to trade disputes between regions, with threats of retaliation and counterretaliation. That would be the more likely outcome over time, as increased imports from intrabloc trading partners might be expected to lead to protectionist pressures against countries outside the bloc, with increases in resort to antidumping and countervailing duties and other measures. While at first countries might resolve those disputes, it is not at all unthinkable that, over time, the degree of acrimony could increase, particularly if there were large bilateral trade imbalances between blocs, for example, the United States and Japan. Moreover, the perceived gains from eschewing a trade war would diminish as intrabloc trade grew and interbloc trade diminished. Trade representatives for the blocs would then become more aggressive in their demands and retaliatory actions.

Even if the evolution of trading blocs began with little or no intent to damage trading relations among blocs, it is certainly likely that trade frictions among blocs would grow over time. As that happened, one or another set of frictions might result in a country's imposing punitive tariffs, which would lead to a cycle of retaliation, counterretaliation, and still higher tariffs by the initiating party.

---

29. The prime minister of Malaysia already proposed that in response to NAFTA. Other East Asian countries, recognizing their strong trading relations with North America, have to date been reluctant to make any commitments to a regional free trade agreement, but at the Asia Pacific Economic Cooperation summit in November 1994, they declared their intention to achieve regional free trade.

30. One immediate concern should then be the fate of the excluded regions, which would presumably include the countries of the former Soviet Union and Eastern Europe, South Asia, the Middle East, and Africa.

There is no inevitability about the emergence of conflicts among regional trading blocs. The European Community for its first thirty years was generally an open, GATT-consistent, trading arrangement, although there were conflicts over agricultural policy and criticisms from EC trading partners that external liberalization was proceeding excessively slowly. EC trade with third countries grew rapidly, despite increasing integration within the community. It thus provides an example of an arrangement that is compatible with GATT principles.

The risk with NAFTA is that protectionist pressures, already using administered protection in the U.S. market, might lead to more antidumping and countervailing duty cases against East Asian and European countries over time to counter other NAFTA members' import penetration in the U.S. market. If antidumping and countervailing duty margins thus increased, either in response to changes toward a more protectionist U.S. Department of Commerce interpretation of its role or for other reasons, East Asian or European retaliation (which has already been threatened in several cases) would inevitably occur at one time or another. Even when disagreements were settled, the legacy of acrimonious trade relations would become stronger. As the cumulative number of disputes mounted, retaliation and counterretaliation would result in permanently increased trade barriers between regions.

That result, in turn, would be deleterious for all countries in the world. As we saw in chapters 1 and 2, the trend toward more liberalized trade has been a major factor underpinning the economic growth at above historical rates since World War II. It is even plausible that the United States, losing its trading linkages with Europe and Japan and relying exclusively on the countries of the Western Hemisphere for its gains from trade, would lose relatively more than either Europe or Asia: a higher fraction of U.S. trade is with countries outside the Western Hemisphere than is Europe's or Japan's trade outside its region. Certainly, in a world of increasingly specialized parts and components, the fragmentation of the world market would raise costs and lower real living standards throughout the world.

Conclusions

NAFTA and any successor Western Hemisphere free trade agreement have the potential for creating a "GATT-plus" preferential trading area, where trade barriers are even lower than they are between the United States and countries that are not members of the Western Hemisphere free trade agreement.

Such a felicitous outcome, however, will hinge crucially on whether the United States manages to support effectively the strengthening of the WTO and the multilateral system and guards against NAFTA or Western Hemisphere free trade agreement arrangements that are incompatible with the open multilateral trading system. The evolution of the regional arrangement will, therefore, be closely related to the degree to which the United States resumes its commitment and leadership in the open multilateral trading system instead of increasing its use of antidumping, countervailing duty, and other trade remedy measures and resorting to bilateral measures and aggressive unilateralism. That is the subject of attention in chapter 6.

6

A Strengthened Multilateral
System or Increased Friction?

With the signing of the Uruguay Round agreement, the world faces an opportunity for increasing still further the liberalization and gains from trade that have spurred economic growth since World War II. In addition to tariff reductions and agreements to reduce agricultural protection, to phase out the Multifiber Arrangement, and to provide for increased access for a number of services, the new World Trade Organization will be established. Its scope will extend beyond the GATT, both because the organization itself will be strengthened (through, for example, an enlarged secretariat) and because the WTO's functions will be extended. Under the WTO, dispute settlement—the slowness of which had been one of the key arguments used to defend U.S. administered protection procedures—should be more effective and speedier than under the GATT. Agreements on other aspects of trade—especially in services—will extend WTO coverage into new, important areas and thus will go far to satisfy the earlier American charge that unilateral action was necessary because of the absence of international agreements covering those issues. There is also the prospect for future trade negotiations under the WTO, with still further strengthening of the multilateral trading system and integration of the world economy.

Estimates of the gains to the world economy from the increased integration achieved under the Uruguay Round agreement vary, but one frequently used number has been an additional $200 billion annually. While there are legitimate grounds for disagreement over the precise magnitude of the gains,[1] there is no disagreement over the proposition that the potential for increased world real GDP resulting from the Uruguay Round agreement can be an important contributor, as well as stimulant, to world economic growth.

At the same time as the Uruguay Round agreement was signed in Marrakesh, however, ominous signs of future difficulty also arose: France and the United States joined forces and announced that unless the Uruguay Round signatories agreed to consideration of labor and environmental codes under the WTO, they would not sign the agreement. After the last-minute triumph in achieving completion of the round, supporters were stunned by that new demand, which had not been voiced during the Uruguay Round negotiations.[2]

Signatories agreed to that condition, and delegates emerged from Marrakesh declaring their task successfully completed. But the tension persists. The official U.S. position is to support the Uruguay Round agreement and the multilateral system. Nevertheless, other U.S. trade practices, including bilateral pressures on the Japanese to accept quantitative indicators of their success in opening their economy for the imports of various goods[3] and on the Canadians with respect to their wheat exports to the United States, as well as the reinstatement of Super 301 and the continuing use of antidumping and countervailing duty procedures against imports as administered protection, give a strong basis for concern about the future direction of U.S. trade policy. Moreover, the United States remains so impor-

---

1. One basis for disagreement is the question as to what the counterfactual is. On one hand, one could assume that in the absence of the Uruguay Round, trade relations and trade barriers will remain the same as in the early 1990s. On the other hand, one could assume that failure to ratify the round would lead to increases in trade barriers and reduced rates of economic growth. There are also the usual difficulties entailed in making any forecast.

2. There had earlier been other disquieting events. During the Uruguay Round negotiations, the United States almost undermined the consensus with respect to trade in services by insisting that maritime shipping, financial services, and basic telecommunications be withdrawn from the protocol providing for MFN treatment of trade in services. In February 1994 the United States had demanded that Japan further lower the tariff on lumber imports, despite the fact that the tariff had been negotiated under the Uruguay Round.

3. In September 1994, as trade talks with the Japanese continued stalemated, the United States even threatened the Japanese with a loss of their MFN privileges in the U.S. market (*Financial Review*, September 14, 1994, p. 14). That this could even be threatened demonstrates how far the United States has come from the days when it was totally committed to the open multilateral system.

tant in the world economy that its further defection from the open multilateral system would seriously detract from the prospects the Uruguay Round opened up and, at a minimum, would weaken the entire international trading system.

It seems useful, therefore, to conclude by assessing the various strands of U.S. trade policy in light of American interests. To do so, I shall briefly evaluate those interests to provide a framework for analysis.

U.S. Concerns with the International System

Three levels of U.S. interest in the international trading system can be distinguished. From the broadest perspective, U.S. policies and actions are an important component of general U.S. relations with the world. It does not require idealism to believe that the United States loses support and influence with respect to its noneconomic objectives when it takes unilateral actions that are inconsistent in spirit, or worse yet even in letter, with previous commitments and that harm another country or countries. Such losses reduce the degree to which the United States can succeed in its nontrade objectives. Analysts must weigh losses from that reduced influence against whatever gains they perceive emanate from trade policies.

At a second level one can analyze alternative global trading systems in light of their impact on the general economic well-being of the American people and the American economy. At that level, analysts can consider both the gains (losses) that may result from a particular action with respect to trade policy and the impact any action has on the international economic system as well as its long-term effects. To make the point, imagine that the United States could impose an optimal tariff on all imports that would immediately increase U.S. real income because of the improved terms of trade. If, however, other countries then began imposing optimal tariffs (and retaliatory tariffs) on their imports and simultaneously reduced imports because of reduced real incomes, the cumulative effect on world trade and world real incomes might be such that the loss to the United States would outweigh the initial gain in terms of trade. In that sense, assessment of any trade action should take into account the repercussions for the United States of any systemic effects U.S. actions might have.

At the third level, analysts can most narrowly assess U.S. interests in trade policy by focusing on the interests of particular groups within the United States, especially groups that are regarded as deserving special consideration. Analysts can then evaluate the impact of trade on those groups. Thus, one can ask which interests gain and which lose and calculate the magnitudes of gains and losses (and alternative means of achieving the same objectives).

U.S. Foreign Policy Concerns. The United States plays a key role in a large number of (noneconomic) global arenas and in particular countries to address its foreign policy concerns. Those range from a desire to have stable, prosperous, and therefore presumably peaceful neighbors all the way to international agreements concerning postal services, air routes, and human rights. Most of those issues require some degree of international cooperation, and it is often in the U.S. interest to act in that context. From those general foreign policy concerns, two conclusions follow.

First, there may be occasions when it would be in the U.S. self-interest to take particular lines of action with respect to trade policy, *even if* those actions were deemed detrimental to the U.S. economic interest. Such was the case, for example, with respect to the U.S. boycott against Cuba after 1959: there was little or no question that damage to U.S. consumers would result, but policy makers deemed it sufficiently in the national interest to isolate Cuba that the United States imposed sanctions anyway.[4] In another example, because of overriding concerns with apartheid, many countries agreed through the United Nations to impose a trade embargo with South Africa although the action imposed economic costs on them.[5]

Trade sanctions through the United Nations are normally much more effective than unilateral measures because of the ease with which reduced trade with the United States can otherwise simply be

---

4. The Cuban situation was unusual in that the United States was the world's largest importer of sugar and had country-specific import quotas on sugar for which Cuba was the largest beneficiary (because the Cubans were entitled to export to the U.S. market at the U.S. price, which was well above the world price). In most situations there are enough alternative sources of supply or demand in the world market that unilateral action is unlikely to be effective.

5. It has often been stated (see, for example, Baldwin (1985)) that American trade policy in the immediate postwar period was based on foreign policy concerns. But that has been taken to imply that an open trading policy was not in U.S. economic interests. In fact, it is almost certainly true that U.S. support for an open multilateral trading system and the American trade policies, although pursued partly because of foreign policy concerns, were very much in the national economic interest.

Concern with foreign policy, however, probably permitted U.S. policy to be formulated with much less regard for special interest groups than would have been the case absent that concern.

replaced with imports from other sources. In the case of South Africa, world opinion was sufficiently in agreement in opposing apartheid that concerted action through the United Nations was possible, and the high degree of consensus made trade sanctions fairly effective. U.N. actions on trade matters supersede GATT and WTO law, and as such provide a multilateral means of using trade policy effectively.

In the 1990s the use of trade policy instruments is once again a significant policy issue. On one hand, questions arise as to whether U.S. trade policy should support other, political, objectives. On the other hand, there are questions as to whether U.S. trade policies, such as administered protection, may not systemically damage the trading system or otherwise impose high indirect costs on U.S. interests.

Turning first to the use of trade policy as an instrument in support of non-trade-related objectives, the considerations were well highlighted in the debate before the U.S. administration decided to renew MFN treatment for China in the winter of 1994.[6] There were two issues. The first was whether the American people were willing to pay the costs they would incur should the Chinese greatly reduce their imports from the United States, as they almost surely would have had to, had denial of MFN treatment drastically reduced their export earnings (as was forecast). The administration decided not to withhold MFN treatment, in large part because there appeared to be an unwillingness to pay that cost.

There was, however, a second issue that policy makers should have considered, even if they had deemed it desirable to pay the costs of withholding MFN treatment from China: whether withholding MFN treatment would induce the Chinese to improve their practices with respect to human rights. Here, too, there were and are serious questions, as many observers believe that the U.S. public focus on those issues led to greater intransigence on the part of the Chinese and that, had MFN treatment been withheld, human rights practices would, if anything, have deteriorated in consequence.

When nations adopt trade policy actions to pursue other goals, a prior question must surely be whether the trade action will succeed in attaining the noneconomic objective.[7] Even when there is a reason-

---

6. At issue were Chinese practices with respect to human rights. Had MFN treatment been denied, it would have been a case in which a noneconomic objective was served by accepting the economic losses associated with the trade penalty.

7. As Bhagwati (1993) has pointed out, there are some who would insist that the United States should in any event incur the cost of its trade action so as not to benefit, even implicitly, by association with the practices deemed

able basis for believing that a trade measure may result in an outcome deemed more desirable from the U.S. viewpoint, it is necessary to ask several questions. First, those in the United States who will benefit from protection are likely to seize any argument that will further their narrow economic self-interest. Therefore, we should ask whether benefits may accrue to those who are advocating a trade policy intervention—allegedly on the grounds of its noneconomic desirability. Second, we may legitimately ask whether there may not be other, less costly means of achieving the same objective, either by using other more effective forums in support of the goal or by resorting to a more effective policy instrument. Finally, we should ask whether the noneconomic objective is truly that. That issue arises most blatantly with respect to concerns expressed over labor markets. Attention returns below to the issues of labor standards and environmental concerns—currently the target for proposed trade policies. As we shall see, all the questions raised here apply to those issues as well.

Turning then to the inverse concern—using trade policy to achieve economic objectives at a cost to other foreign policy concerns—a first important question about which much was written in earlier chapters is whether restrictive trade policies are in the national economic interest. But, for purposes of discussion, I focus here on an issue or issues on which the United States would gain economic benefits at the cost of other foreign policy objectives.

When the Bush administration decided that it would oppose the Iraqi invasion of Kuwait, it felt the strong need for other countries' support. Policies with respect to all aspects of international relations surely affected other countries' decisions as to whether and to what extent to support the administration. Trade relations were doubtless among those considerations.[8]

Even if there were national or sectoral economic interests for protection that would be politically supported, a first question should be whether the economic objectives can be achieved in a way that is less costly to general diplomacy. In many instances the clear-cut

---

abhorrent. Most rhetoric, however, has focused on the desirability of using trade policy to "force" others to eschew unacceptable practices.

8. In at least one instance, the trade link was made quite explicit. Turkish support for the Gulf War was deemed of great importance both because of Turkey's strategic location and because of the felt need to demonstrate that the action was not simply the West against a Muslim country. The Turkish president, Turgut Ozel, rapidly indicated his willingness to support the effort, but asked for a larger quota for Turkish exports of textiles and apparel to the United States under the Multifiber Arrangement.

conclusion is that trade actions through multilateral forums have a significantly lower cost (and may even have net benefits) in terms of the international political losses associated with unilateral American actions. When U.S. trade policy is conducted bilaterally and outside the agreed-upon (spirit or letter of the) international trading system, one must evaluate whatever benefits are deemed to come from such a derogation relative to the gain-loss calculus that would ensue from multilateral pursuits of the same objective. In most instances one can convincingly argue that the costs would be significantly less through multilateral forums.[9]

Quite aside from the economic damage U.S. protectionist policies inflict on Americans, especially when those policies are undertaken outside the multilateral system, policy makers must consider the foreign policy consequences. Some of those, such as the degree to which the open multilateral trading system functions smoothly and the extent of international monetary cooperation, are themselves economic variables of concern to the United States. But other variables must be of concern simply because political relations with the country in question are important. Thus, President Clinton extended MFN treatment to China because of the country's importance and despite the Chinese intransigence with respect to the human rights issues that were the focal point of disagreement.[10]

Good political relations with Japan are important for many reasons, not least of which in the early 1990s was anxiety over North Korea. *Even if* the issues the United States raised with Japan were in the U.S. economic self-interest, one could legitimately question whether they were in the general U.S. self-interest, given the importance of noneconomic relations with that country.

Those foreign policy concerns should also influence American trade policy with respect to Europe. There, issues of importance, such as the emergence of Eastern Europe and the states of the former Soviet Union and conflict in the Balkans, surely are ample reason for desiring amicable relations.

Analysts and journalists have often noted that U.S. bilateral trade policy seems to become more aggressive with respect to smaller U.S. trading partners than with respect to larger ones. The United States

---

9. In addition, of course, many of the trade policy objectives that have been sought bilaterally have failed to be met because of third-country considerations. Resort to multilateral forums can avoid this pitfall.

10. In the case of China, part of the reason for the failure to withdraw MFN treatment was concern that U.S. export interests in such a large country would be damaged.

even treats Japan and Europe (which is arguably as protectionist as Japan, if not more so) differently. The greater U.S. bargaining power with Japan is likely due to Europe's greater ability to retaliate and to the greater importance of the United States to Japan. But the contrast between U.S. pressures on Japan and those on smaller trading nations, such as Korea, is even more pronounced. Other nations greatly resent the "bullying" of small trading nations, and the practice imposes a cost when other issues of concern to the United States arise.

The desirability of conducting trade policy in ways that least damage other U.S. foreign policy interests is in itself a powerful argument for handling trade relations multilaterally. Bilateral negotiations inevitably accentuate acrimony. Conversely, when the United States can appeal to an international institution under internationally agreed-on standards as a basis for complaining about a trading partner's trading practices, the potential losses with respect to other aspects of international relations are considerably smaller than they are when the approach is bilateral and outside the GATT and the WTO. In and of itself, therefore, it is in the U.S. self-interest to pursue its legitimate concerns with respect to trading partners' practices through international forums and under international agreements, insofar as possible.

National Economic Interests. The fundamental fact, however, is that U.S. national economic interests lie largely with the pursuit of free trade. In recent years much political discussion of U.S. trade policy has lost sight of that point.

Virtually all the arguments made against a policy of free trade do not, in fact, withstand scrutiny when examined in light of the prevailing pattern of protection.[11] Some, related to environmental considerations, make a case for policy intervention domestically and internationally: those I further discuss below. Others are arguments for restricting trade because it will benefit a particular group or groups in society. In many of those instances, the protection-seeking interests are not those with which the body politic has great sympathy. Advocates expend a great deal of effort putting forth arguments that may have public appeal but do not withstand scrutiny and making protection in those instances as opaque as possible. Those instances of protection usually benefit the well-off few at the expense of those deemed more deserving of social support. In addition, they are often precisely the measures that most antagonize U.S. trading partners and have high economic costs (see chapter 2).

---

11. See chapter 2 for an elaboration of that point.

To be sure, there can be legitimate concerns with income distribution and the fate of the relatively unskilled. I further discuss worries with respect to the impact of free trade on unskilled workers below. In virtually all such instances of legitimate social concern, one can readily demonstrate that there are economically cheaper ways of achieving the same goals. Since, in those circumstances, protectionist measures hurt U.S. foreign policy objectives and the entire U.S. economy, and since alternative policies to achieve the same objectives at lower cost are available, the argument for trade intervention is weak.

Even when advocates of intervention cited considerations of national defense during the cold war era, one could raise serious questions. For example, those advocates often asserted that the United States needed its own high-tech industries (especially computers) so that it would not be dependent on foreign supplies in the event of military hostilities. The difficulty with that argument, of course, was that the very presumption that protection might be needed for an industry deemed crucial for defense implied that the U.S. military would rely on lower quality or otherwise inferior hardware contrasted with that available in the international market.[12] Even when advocates of protection argue that the United States should secure the domestic availability of a particular item to be sure of access to it if war should occur, options such as stockpiling or mothballing production capabilities can be low-cost alternatives to protecting a domestic industry's high-cost production.[13]

Support for Particular Groups. Particular groups seek most trade policy interventions, however, because of their own special circumstances. In many instances one can cogently and even conclusively argue that yielding to their demands serves little or no national purpose and that protection may not even achieve beneficial results for the industry over the longer term.

One legitimate concern, however, relates to declining industries.

---

12. Indeed, for years, many European governments supported companies in their countries as "national champions" by arguing that the domestic presence of such industries was vital. Experience in those cases suggested that those champions were also-rans internationally and that the policies fostered high-cost, generally low-quality producers.

13. Until the 1960s, there were even oil import quotas, on the grounds that the United States needed to maintain a flow of oil output to be assured of supplies in the event of wartime! More serious analysis would have suggested that the appropriate policy for that end would have been to tax domestic production to keep oil in the ground in the event foreign oil became unavailable due to hostilities. See Dam (1971).

Criteria for relief under administered protection provisions include some degree of "damage" to the industry, but sympathy for those who may potentially become unemployed is often a powerful political argument in support of protection. In those cases policy makers need to weigh several considerations. A first is whether protection effectively alleviates the hardships that evoke sympathy contrasted with retraining programs, adjustment assistance, or other measures that directly improve the lot of the workers at risk. In the cases of automobiles, steel, and textiles and apparel, employment in each industry has decreased *despite* protection.

Several factors lead to such a result. Industries in serious difficulty that seek protection of jobs normally face several adverse conditions: productivity is rising rapidly; demand is rising slowly; and imports are increasing (and exports decreasing). In consequence, imports are only one source of dislocation. Usually they contribute less to general problems than popular discussion and appeals for protection suggest. If the government accords or increases protection for an industry subject to those difficulties, it can in most instances do little more than slow down the rate of decline in employment. Thus, we must view protection as doing nothing more than delaying (and presumably therefore easing) the industry's adjustment. One can then legitimately ask whether the high costs of protection per job temporarily "saved" are worth the expenditures, relative to alternative measures not involving trade policy that can achieve the same result.

A second type of appeal for trade policy intervention has come from some high-tech industries: the semiconductor industry has been the most visible. Here advocates argue that the industry must survive in the United States because of its importance to further productivity gains across a range of industries. That argument, too, must evoke considerable skepticism. Any country whose industries must rely on higher cost or lower quality products than foreign competitors' surely inflicts great harm on the national economy. That is certainly true of the high-tech industries for which protection is sometimes sought. While there may be a case for supporting generic research and development or possibly even for educating the labor force and providing them training, one cost of protecting goods that are essential inputs to other production processes is bound to be the loss of competitiveness by a wide variety of industries.

Some analysts have argued that the "market-opening" aspect of VIEs, such as that under the semiconductor agreement, is in some sense "better" than protection because it expands trade. In fact, powerful considerations lead to the conclusion that such a claim is false.[14]

---

14. See Irwin (1994), on whose arguments this paragraph is based.

First, there are significant issues as to the effect of such "market-opening" agreements on the industry-government relationship in the importing country. To assure compliance with quantitative import targets, government officials must have mechanisms to induce domestic firms to increase imports. Clearly, the negotiated VERs and VIEs with Japan strengthened MITI and enabled the Japanese industry to behave collusively. Second, there is no widely accepted basis for ascertaining what the quantitative target "should" be. Third, "market-opening" VIEs are inherently bilateral and thus damage third countries.[15] Fourth, divorcing "demands" for market opening from any imperative for the United States reciprocally to reduce any of its own trade barriers significantly diminishes the political pressures restraining increases in protection. Once potential and actual exporters believe that they can achieve their market-opening objectives without the necessity for reciprocal liberalization in the United States, their incentives to support the open multilateral system and U.S. trade liberalization are significantly reduced.[16]

Farm groups have been another special interest seeking protection. Especially when American farm incomes are low, farmers' organizations have appealed to the American public for support for the family farm. That has struck a responsive chord that provided the basis for a receptive political response. In addition to those concerns, farm organizations have sought protection on the grounds that European and Japanese support for their agriculture is unfair and on grounds that failure to provide protection would increase the cost of U.S. farm programs.

While it is certainly true that European and Japanese support for agriculture has increased subsidized exports and has hence put downward pressure on world prices, the United States has not been entirely innocent. Indeed, the United States has an Export Enhancement Program (that provides direct subsidies for exports of several commodities, of which the most important is wheat), a sugar program, restrictions on imports of meat, and supports for cotton, to-

---

15. As we saw in chapter 4, the semiconductor agreement with Japan had many third-country consequences. American computer assemblers protested because they were forced to pay more for their chips; Europeans protested; and Korean producers were enabled to enter the market sooner than they otherwise would have. See Irwin (forthcoming) for an account.

16. There are even reports of instances when the USTR was bargaining for market access that would have affected only one U.S. firm. While the bargaining was in session, a representative of that firm was in an adjoining room, and the USTR periodically checked with him to ensure that the resulting bargain was "satisfactory." See Irwin (forthcoming) for more details.

bacco, peanuts, rice, dairy products, and a number of other commodities.

As with other pleas for protection, the government can show sympathy for farmers without resorting to protection. Deficiency payments for farmers provide a less costly means than protection for supplementing farm incomes. Even for legitimate concerns about the effect of other countries' protection on agricultural prices, negotiation for multilateral liberalization of agricultural trade is a solution far superior to increased protection with export subsidies for U.S. farmers.

Simultaneously dismantling support regimes for European, Japanese, and American agriculture will significantly reduce the adjustment costs for each region relative to those that would be incurred with unilateral reduction of support for agriculture. Progress in the Uruguay Round with respect to agriculture was significant, especially with regard to undertakings that there would be tariffication of existing border measures and that farm income support programs would be designed that would not lead to increased production incentives.

Current Trends in U.S. Trade Policy

Viewed from any perspective—foreign policy concerns, national economic interest, or sympathy for the plight of a particular group—there are good reasons for questioning the efficacy of protectionism and other bilateral or unilateral trade interventions, especially when they are unilaterally imposed. Nonetheless, as already seen, schizophrenia in American trade policy continues.

The 1994 *Economic Report of the President* (1994, 233–36) wrote enthusiastically of the Uruguay Round results and noted that the "stakes . . . were enormous." It welcomed the advent of the World Trade Organization. It listed areas in which the United States had achieved a great deal: integrating agriculture; liberalizing textiles and apparel and phasing out the MFA; bringing trade in services, investment, and intellectual property rights further under the WTO discipline; reforming dispute settlement procedures; strengthening agreements circumscribing the use of export subsidies; replacing nontariff barriers with tariffs (tariffication); and, of course, reducing tariffs.

As all who have considered trade policy know, many of the issues about which there are stated U.S. concerns are inherently multilateral: most imports to the United States originate from many countries, and most efforts to deal bilaterally are therefore bound to be at best partially effective. For textiles and apparel and agriculture, two sectors of great concern to American politicians, multilateral liberalization will greatly benefit U.S. interests, while unilateral American liberalization would pose considerably greater adjustment burdens on the industries. For U.S. export interests, maintaining an open world trading system is vitally important, and even for import-competing interests narrowly viewed, international competition is largely healthy. From the perspective of the entire economy, it is vital.

Yet, as seen in preceding chapters, the United States, while expressing support for the multilateral system, acts in ways that tend to undermine it. Administered protection as currently practiced, bilateral pressures and negotiations with Japan, Korea, and others, and Super 301 detract from the multilateral system. In addition, there is confusion among U.S. trading partners as to the direction the United States will take with respect to NAFTA and other regional approaches.

A Trade Policy Agenda for the United States

On the basis of considerations of general national (foreign policy) interest, national economic interests, and even most sectoral interests, U.S. trade policy needs rethinking. Perhaps the most important action would be a negative one: the United States could achieve much by removing some of the practices that most irritate its trading partners and that derogate from the multilateral system. The United States could make significant progress in achieving that objective by further correcting its fiscal imbalances. On the positive side, the United States should support and strengthen the new WTO to maximize the effectiveness of its new dispute settlement procedures and other functions. Other actions would also help: the United States could amend its antidumping and countervailing duty procedures in ways that make them more consistent with the stated goals and less protectionist in effect. Statements and actions could reflect the commitment of the United States to maintain its preferential trading arrangement in a "WTO-plus" manner. Finally, policies and policy pronouncements with respect to labor standards and environmental concerns should be formulated in ways that do not permit their capture by protectionist interests and that are consistent with an open multilateral trading system.

Support for the WTO. While the WTO is taking shape, U.S. trade policy should clearly and virtually exclusively focus on providing an environment as favorable as possible for the launching of the new institution. Instead, debates in Congress center on the "loss of sovereignty" implicit in enabling WTO dispute settlement procedures to be strengthened (despite earlier statements that the United States had to act bilaterally because of the absence of such procedures). As late as November 1994, there was even some doubt as to whether Congress would approve the Uruguay Round in time for the WTO to begin its existence according to the Uruguay Round timetable on January 1, 1995.

Eschew Bilateral Demands and Negotiations. Although the agreement was ratified, there are several threats to the system. First and foremost, there are continuing bilateral disputes that bypass the GATT and the WTO and for reasons discussed in earlier chapters therefore weaken the open multilateral system.

In the winter of 1994–95, the most publicized and dangerous of those disputes was with Japan, where the threat of the U.S. administration's imposing Super 301 at the end of September 1994 could lead to a grievous bilateral escalation in trade tensions.[17] That the removal of MFN privileges was even suggested indicates the extent to which the United States is willing to depart from its earlier principles with respect to the system. While it is reasonable to assume that the threatened removal of MFN privileges was a bargaining ploy, even the suggestion raises questions as to the U.S. commitment to the open multilateral system in the minds of many in the rest of the world.

Ratification of the Uruguay Round, removal of the Super 301 threat with Japan, and resolution of the bilateral difficulties precipitated by U.S. demands for "quantitative indicators" with respect to insurance, auto parts, and other U.S. exports would be a promising start for improving the prospects for the world trading system. Attempting to shift trade disputes away from bilateral forums and toward the WTO would then signal the renewal of the U.S. commitment to multilateralism and the WTO.

---

17. In mid-September 1994, Sir Leon Brittan, the European trade commissioner, listed a series of trade outcomes that were believed to have been discriminatory against Europe as a result of U.S. "demands" and bargaining with Japan. Instances reported in the newspapers as being among the European complaints included: increases in Japanese imports of U.S. autos and auto parts with a simultaneous drop in imports of those items from European sources; Japanese purchases of Boeing aircraft without consideration given to the Airbus alternative; Japan's failure to use Rolls-Royce engines for its airline fleets; and exemption of U.S. medical equipment from inspection procedures still applied to similar European-sourced equipment (*Financial Times*, September 14, 1994, p. 3). There were also serious disputes between the United States and China, although China was not yet in the WTO.

Correct Macroeconomic Imbalances. As I showed in chapter 2, a country's current account balance represents the excess of domestic expenditures over domestic income, which is to say that domestic investment exceeds domestic savings. When the current account is in deficit, that can mean that domestic savings are simply inadequate to cover desired (and profitable) investments. Or, it can occur because savings are low (either because private savings are low or because government expenditures exceed government revenues and the excess is financed by private savings and capital inflows).

For the United States there is little evidence that the rate of investment is unusually high.[18] Moreover, in the 1980s the increase in the American current account deficit coincided with a jump in the U.S. fiscal deficit. Indeed, as the U.S. fiscal deficit fell as a percentage of GDP in the late 1980s, so did the current account deficit.

While the linkage between the fiscal deficit and the current account deficit is not exact, it is nonetheless strong. The United States, as a rich, capital-abundant country, probably should be a net exporter of capital to the rest of the world. To achieve that would, however, require more action with respect to prospective fiscal deficits (and possibly other measures to encourage savings and perhaps reduce investment) than politicians have so far been willing to undertake.

Given current fiscal policy, it makes little sense to focus on the current account balance as an independent objective of policy, and especially not on bilateral trade balances with individual countries. Even if the Japanese decided to encourage imports (for example, by subsidizing imports by a given percentage), the extent to which their current account balance would be affected would depend on whether the subsidy increased current consumption. To the extent that Japanese savings and investment behavior was unaffected, yen depreciation would offset any increase in imports. And there is little basis on which to presume that trade policy changes affect savings and investment behavior.

Even if such a subsidy did increase Japanese domestic consumption at the expense of savings and thus reduced the Japanese current account balance, that reduction would affect Japan's global balance: as such, current account deficits of countries such as Korea would diminish, along with the U.S. current account deficit. To the extent that happened, worldwide interest rates would need to rise to offset the reduction in worldwide savings.[19]

---

18. It is true, however, that if foreigners had not been willing to acquire U.S. assets in exchange for their goods and services in the 1980s, domestic investment would have been "crowded out" to a greater extent than it was.

19. See McCullogh (1994) for an analysis.

Reduction in the American current account deficit would almost surely reduce political pressures on U.S. trade policy officials to engage in bilateral negotiations with countries whose accounts are in bilateral surplus. The period during which the American current account deficit rose in the early 1980s was, not surprisingly, the period during which protectionist pressures increased, administered protection law was strengthened and came to be used with greater frequency, and bilateral "trade talks" with Japan, Korea, and other countries became such prominent features of U.S. trade policy.

Reducing the size of the American fiscal, and therefore the current account, deficit would contribute greatly to reducing protectionist pressures and sentiment in the United States. Despite the fact that fiscal policy is not trade policy, a fiscal policy action might have more significant consequences for trade policy than any direct trade policy measures that may be contemplated. Clearly, fiscal policy should not be based on trade policy any more than trade policy should be used to achieve a variety of other objectives. But, insofar as the current stance of American fiscal policy is deemed harmful to the U.S. economy, the protectionist pressures that the U.S. current account deficit further increases make yet one more reason for policy measures to reduce the fiscal deficit.

Amend Trade Remedy Procedures and Criteria. As we have seen in earlier chapters, administered protection procedures and processes are a major irritant to foreigners and provide a mechanism whereby protection seekers in the United States can reasonably hope to attain protection.

The recent administration of trade remedy legislation has had strong protectionist and bilateral overtones with two aspects. First, the antidumping and countervailing duty findings and tariffs in and of themselves have been protectionist. Second, American industries have used the antidumping and countervailing duty processes as a lever. The filing of cases has prodded the American administration and foreign governments to agree to voluntary export restraints in preference to risking the outcome of the legal proceedings, which are, in ways noted in chapter 3, biased against foreign producers in unpredictable ways.

Voluntary export restraints are, by their nature, inherently bilateral and contravene the essential features of an open multilateral trading system.[20] With the inauguration of the WTO, "tariffication" of

---

20. An argument could also be made that VERs have not achieved the objectives of those seeking protection and have, on several occasions, actually

existing nontariff barriers to trade is contemplated. As that takes place, voluntary export restraints—most important, the Multifiber Arrangement—should gradually disappear. That would still leave American administered protection as a major irritant to U.S. trading partners. U.S. industries would increasingly resort to that avenue once VERs were infeasible, unless changes were made.

Trade remedy law has legitimate objectives. They are to prevent predatory pricing, sudden serious injury resulting from a "burst" of imports, and large-scale state subsidies to obtain "first-mover" advantage. But the United States can realize those objectives without the massive costs in ill will and capricious protection that currently result from antidumping and countervailing duty trade remedies.[21]

First, within the WTO, the subsidies code and procedures for dispute resolution about subsidies can be strengthened.[22] That would strengthen the multilateral system and permit equal treatment of U.S. trading partners (rather than the present appearance of arbitrary discrimination among countries based on the nature of the evidence supplied). Taking complaints over subsidies to the WTO, rather than using U.S. processes, could do much not only to provide remedies, but to discourage countries from using subsidies in the first place.

Second, the United States could alter administered protection procedures in ways that would make them less conducive to seizure for protectionist purposes and nonetheless permit them to perform their intended functions against practices deemed to be unfair. The Department of Commerce itself could alter several procedures without any new law. Those include the requirements for format of data

---

injured the American producers, who were the supposed beneficiaries. While industry representatives might contend that this failure was the result of insufficiently restrictive VERs, it can also be argued that the third-party effects (for example, Korean semiconductors, new entrants into textiles and apparel, Hyundai and European automobile producers at the expense of the Japanese), and increased profitability of exporting firms in the targeted countries, have accounted for that result.

21. The industrial organization literature recognizes that predatory pricing can occur in two ways: either a firm may engage in it with intent to monopolize and profit later or a firm may use the legal process to inhibit potential competitors. It is likely that U.S. administered protection provides the legal framework in which some deterrence to foreign competitors does occur. See OECD (1989).

22. Although during the Uruguay Round parties agreed on a stronger subsidies code, the United States announced that it did not wish to sign that code. Instead, the United States preferred to retain its option to provide subsidies to U.S. producers and exporters.

submission, the criteria for rejecting observations, and a number of other practices that bias antidumping, countervailing duty, and escape clause administration.[23]

Even more should be done, however. One important step would be to raise "de minimis" standards, so that antidumping or countervailing duty margins of, say, at least 10 percent would be necessary for a positive finding. The enabling legislation for the Uruguay Round is disappointing in that regard. The de minimis margin for antidumping cases is raised to only 2 percent.

Another measure would be to change the law to conform more closely to the economists' notion of predatory pricing, possibly by making a finding of dumping contingent on the exporter's having sold below *marginal* cost. An alternative that would go far to accomplish the same objective would be to subject foreign firms' pricing practices for the U.S. market to the same standards that are applied to American firms under U.S. law. That would, in effect, place foreign and domestic sellers of a product under the same standard. Such a change in itself would remove a great deal of the bias inherent in current trade remedy administration.[24]

In the interest of the American economy, as well as the international economic system, an even more desirable change would be to alter the mandate of the USITC so that it was instructed to consider the impact of any tariffs imposed not from the viewpoint of the industry claiming a grievance, but from the perspective of the economy as a whole. Such a change would permit users of imported products prospectively subject to escape clause action to present evidence with respect to the potential effects on them. It would also invite users' groups more generally to recognize their interest in protection.

All of those changes would reduce the protectionism inherent in current U.S. administrative trade remedy procedures. Most of them would cause U.S. practices to conform more closely with those of the GATT and the WTO. They would also reduce the tendency, already apparent, for other countries to emulate the U.S. laws and to use their antidumping and countervailing duty legislation and practices to protect domestic industry. If those changes were made, they could significantly reduce the protectionist effect of U.S. administered trade remedy, while simultaneously retaining defenses against possible extremes.

---

23. See Boltuck and Litan (1991b) for an account.
24. Under current U.S. law, U.S. exporters are exempt from the laws governing pricing behavior in the U.S. market.

Ensure That Regional Trading Arrangements Are WTO-Consistent.
One of the most difficult issues in trade policy is the relationship
between regional and global trading arrangements. When regional
arrangements are designed to further integrate several economies
within the context of a liberalized trade regime under the WTO, they
may contribute significantly to global trade liberalization. But when
they are used to promote regional trade at the expense of third countries (or to divert support from multilateral arrangements), they can
undermine the open multilateral system.

Experience with the European trading arrangement illustrates
elements of both those tendencies. On one hand, trade in industrial
goods was liberalized externally as well as internally, so that European imports from the rest of the world grew fivefold from the 1950s
to the 1980s, while intra-European imports grew eightfold. On the
other hand, the Common Agricultural Policy was clearly a trade-
diverting arrangement that increased trade barriers vis-à-vis the rest
of the world.

To date, all policy pronouncements and actions with respect to
NAFTA have signaled the U.S. intent to undertake preferential trading arrangements as a "WTO-plus" arrangement, consistent with all
obligations under the WTO. It is to be hoped that such is the case,
and there are no reasons in principle why it cannot be.

Nonetheless, a number of issues are unresolved. Perhaps the
most important are the conditions under which other countries will
be permitted or encouraged to enter into a free trade agreement with
the United States. If each new entrant is essentially dealt with bilaterally (as is already the case with Canadian and Mexican agriculture
vis-à-vis the United States), there are significant dangers that a com-
plicated "hub-and-spoke" system could emerge with complex trading
arrangements. As additional countries seek membership in a free
trade agreement with the United States, questions as to the terms
on which new members will be accepted will become increasingly
important. One question already raised is whether membership is
restricted to countries in the Western Hemisphere.

A second concern that has been voiced focuses on the potential
use of administered protection against third countries when imports
into the United States increase from a NAFTA trading partner. Revi-
sion of the trade remedy laws along the lines suggested above would
mitigate that danger to some extent, but some U.S. trading partners
(especially in East Asia) have voiced concern that their exports might
be subject to antidumping or countervailing duty suits should U.S.
imports from NAFTA countries increase significantly.

A third issue arises from the U.S. initiative with APEC (Asia

Pacific Economic Cooperation) under which there has been a declaration that the region will become one of free trade by the year 2020, with industrialized countries' achieving that objective by 2010. The declaration is ambiguous: if it means that all countries in the region will practice free trade, that is completely consistent with GATT and WTO principles and will strengthen the open multilateral system.

If, however, it means that there will be a preferential trading area within the region, many questions can be raised. They include the relationship between preferences extended by APEC members which are also in NAFTA to preferences under NAFTA. Clearly, free trade would have to be across all sectors; if that can be achieved under APEC, including the United States and Japan, a question arises as to why it cannot be achieved globally. Finally, the way in which the free trade agreement was implemented, including rules of origin, would be important. In free trade agreements rules of origin assume importance as possible protectionist measures. Should the United States expand the number of countries with which it has such agreements, it should ensure that the provisions regarding rules of origin and other arrangements do not divert trade from third countries.

The Question of Labor Standards. As already noted, the United States and France announced that they would not sign the Marrakesh agreement unless there was an undertaking to consider adoption of a labor standards code under the WTO. Calls for labor standards have been heard repeatedly in postwar years. The argument has been put forth that working conditions in other countries—especially poor developing countries—are very bad, and that it is "unfair" for U.S. (and, as the argument is heard in Europe, European) firms to have to compete with products made under those conditions.

The argument is a dangerous one. Just as the United States derives much of its comparative advantage from its abundance of highly educated and trained workers and its capital stock, so too do poor developing countries derive much of their comparative advantage from their relative abundance of unskilled labor. Indeed, those developing countries that have grown very rapidly have started their development at a time when their real wages were very low. They have exported goods intensive in the use of unskilled labor, thereby expanding employment and real incomes. Over time, as workers have gained experience and as educational standards have risen (which was possible in part because of higher real incomes resulting from exports), real wages have risen and comparative advantage has shifted away from highly labor-intensive goods.

In the early stages of development, real wages are low because

121

labor productivity is low. It is only the fact of low real wages that enables firms in poor developing countries to compete in international markets. While those workers' poverty, low productivity,[25] low wages, and poor working conditions are deplorable, refusal to accept imports from countries in which wages are low would be tantamount to dooming unskilled workers to perpetual poverty and the countries to much slower economic development.

Rich Americans and Europeans discover how low wages are in developing countries and immediately conclude that there is something "unfair" about labor markets in those countries. Yet, while it is certainly "unfair" that anyone should receive low wages, factory workers in most developing countries receive above-average wages, and laborers queue for jobs in those factories.

In the American debate, it has been asserted that labor is "exploited" in developing countries and that wages are artificially suppressed. If that were the case, one would observe conditions of excess demand for labor. But, as anyone who has traveled to a developing country knows, there is usually a large excess supply of labor.[26]

Officials in a large number of developing countries have vigorously opposed the imposition of "labor standards" as part of the WTO. There are significant dangers that calls for labor standards, which understandably evoke a responsive chord from those who cannot imagine living standards as low as they are in many developing countries, might in fact result in even greater poverty, or at least in a reduced rate of improvement in living standards.

Moreover, those in labor-intensive industries (including employers) have been quick to seize the "unfair labor conditions" argument and to advocate highly restrictive standards. We should clearly recognize that restrictive labor standards would protect labor-intensive in-

---

25. During the NAFTA debate, Hufbauer and Schott (1992) calculated that unit labor costs in the United States were actually slightly lower than they were in Mexico. In other words, despite the huge differential in wages between the two countries, American workers' productivity exceeded that of Mexican workers by more than the wage differential. The only way in the long run to increase living standards in poor countries is to experience increases in productivity. Those will come about less rapidly if the countries do not have access to the markets of the developed countries.

26. Questions have also been raised concerning prison and child labor. There is already an international protocol for prison labor. The issue of child labor is vexed: there are legitimate issues of intolerable working conditions, but employment of children may provide food that prevents a family from starving. In some instances, also, it may provide girls with an alternative to forced early marriages.

dustries in the countries with a comparative advantage in skill- and capital-intensive industries, and that calls from those quarters for labor standards are equivalent to calls for protection. That many labor unions in developing countries oppose those proposals for labor standards attests to the extent to which advocacy is based on protectionist concerns, rather than on the welfare of workers in developing countries.

It is vitally important for world economic growth that legitimate concerns with labor standards be clearly separated from the calls for enforcing measures that would deny developing countries their comparative advantage.

Environmental Issues. The issue of trade policy in relation to labor standards is for the most part analytically fairly straightforward, especially when contrasted with environmental issues. But, in the case of the environment as well as with labor, there are significant dangers that legitimate concerns will be (or are being) seized by those who recognize that measures undertaken in the name of the environment would provide protection for them.

Environmental concerns clearly increase in importance as people become richer.[27] Many of the developed countries spoiled their own environments in the course of their development. But there are significant dangers when officials from affluent, industrialized countries attempt to impose their environmental desires or standards on poorer countries. A key issue with respect to the environment is to ensure that measures that are taken are indeed effective: that argues very strongly for environmental action through multilateral organizations rather than in bilateral negotiations between the United States and individual poor countries.

Economists' analysis of the environment has started by pointing out that there are two kinds of environmentally damaging activities: those that adversely affect the environment worldwide, such as chlorofluorocarbons, and those that adversely affect the environment only in the country in which the activity occurs. The former require the development of a global regime. With respect to the latter set of activities, if rich countries are rich enough to want to bear the costs

---

27. Aside from the fact that developing countries will understandably refuse to give up their developmental objectives because of environmental concerns, it should be remembered that as growth occurs, people in developing countries not only will attach more weight to the desirability of a better environment, but will also have more resources to deal with environmental issues.

of maintaining a cleaner environment, while poor countries choose to spend their resources on other activities, one can argue that differences in costs of doing business because of those environmental concerns are a legitimate part of comparative advantage: locating polluting activities in poor countries enables an "exchange" of more income for a cleaner environment. The argument for "protection" to offset the higher costs in rich countries does not withstand scrutiny. Protection simply enables increased pollution (or higher cleanup costs) in the rich country.

For activities generating international environmental spillovers, of course, there must in any event be an international regime, as is the case with chlorofluorocarbons. A major difficulty in arriving at such a regime arises precisely because developing countries perceive that they are entitled to their "share" of pollution rights on the basis of population and their future income prospects; most citizens of rich countries take their existing share of world production and pollution as a starting point.

Trade policy cannot and should not address those difficult issues; international agreements are the appropriate means for doing so. Having developed such agreements, subscribing nations could agree to impose trade sanctions against violators of those agreements. To attempt through U.S. trade policy to deal unilaterally with other countries' polluting activities is likely to risk trade conflicts without improving environmental prospects.

Conclusions

Much of current U.S. trade policy is bilateral in nature and often protectionist. Yet it is strongly in the U.S. interest that there be an open multilateral trading system. If the United States persists in its bilateral and protectionist policies, the system will inevitably be affected. The United States is simply too important a trading nation to be able to derogate from the system without other countries' responding to its actions.

Much of the rhetoric about Japan, the "unfairness" of trade, and other justifications for bilateralism and protectionism originates from those seeking protection for their own narrow interests. Many of the allegations do not bear close scrutiny; even those that have some substance seldom warrant the sorts of protectionist responses that are advocated.

With the WTO beginning its institutional life, most of the legitimate American concerns regarding the global trading system can be addressed through multilateral forums. Perpetuating unilateral bargaining, designating trading partners as "unfair," and bypassing the multilateral system can harm the U.S. as well as the entire world's economy in the longer run.

Just as economists were coming to grips with such issues, advocates of protection have been joined by those concerned about labor standards and environmental issues. With respect to labor standards, there is little reason to believe that the argument is anything other than yet another protectionist appeal.

Environmental issues are more difficult. Economic analysis, however, provides an important insight: when there is a noneconomic objective or market failure, the first-best policy for meeting the objective or offsetting the failure will not be a trade policy intervention; intervening at the source will achieve a result as good, if not better, at lower cost. In the case of environmental objectives, trade policy is very likely to be a totally ineffective instrument for achieving those objectives and might even backfire. Seeking multilateral agreements directly addressing environmental issues is a much more promising path.

The fundamental proposition that free trade is the best policy still stands. American policy has been dangerously schizophrenic on the issue for over a decade. The world, and the United States, are fortunate that, to date, the damage to the global system has been small. It is time, however, for the United States to reassert the importance of multilateral approaches to trade issues and to provide its strong support for the open multilateral trading system.

References

Anderson, Keith B. 1993. "Antidumping Laws in the United States: Use and Welfare Consequences." *Journal of World Trade* 27 (April).

Auerbach, Stuart. 1990. "Mexico Comes Calling for Free Trade." *Washington Post*, June 19, p. H1.

Baldwin, Richard, and Paul Krugman. 1988. "Industrial Policy and International Competition in Wide-Bodied Jet Aircraft." In Robert E. Baldwin, ed., *Trade Policy Issues and Empirical Analysis*. Chicago: University of Chicago Press, pp. 45–71.

Baldwin, Robert E. 1970. *Nontariff Distortions of International Trade*. Washington, D.C.: Brookings Institution.

Baldwin, Robert E. 1985. *The Political Economy of U.S. Import Policy*. Cambridge: MIT Press.

Baldwin, Robert E. 1988. *Trade Policy in a Changing World Economy*. Chicago: University of Chicago Press.

Baldwin, Robert E., Tain-Jy Chen, and Douglas Nelson. 1995. *Political Economy of U.S.-Taiwan Trade Relations*. Ann Arbor: University of Michigan Press.

Beltz, Cynthia. 1991. *High-Tech Maneuvers: Industrial Policy Lessons of HDTV*. Washington: AEI Press.

Bhagwati, Jagdish N. 1993. "Trade and the Environment: The False Conflict?" Bradley lecture. Washington, D.C.: American Enterprise Institute.

Bhagwati, Jagdish N., and Hugh T. Patrick, eds. 1990. *Aggressive Unilateralism: America's 301 Trade Policy and the World Trading System*. Ann Arbor: University of Michigan Press.

Boltuck, Richard D. 1993. "The Material Injury Determination in Unfair Trade Cases: The U.S. Experience with Competing Analytical

Approaches." Washington, D.C.: Trade Resources Company, October.

Boltuck, Richard D., and Robert E. Litan. 1991a. "America's 'Unfair' Trade Laws." In Richard D. Boltuck and Robert E. Litan, eds., *Down in the Dumps: Administration of the Unfair Trade Laws*. Washington, D.C.: Brookings Institution, pp. 1–22.

Boltuck, Richard D., and Robert E. Litan, eds. 1991b. *Down in the Dumps: Administration of the Unfair Trade Laws*. Washington, D.C.: Brookings Institution.

Bovard, James. 1991a. *The Fair Trade Fraud*. New York: St. Martin's Press.

Bovard, James. 1991b. "America's Most Harebrained Import Quota." *Wall Street Journal*, October 11, p. A8.

Chin, Judith, and Gene Grossman. 1990. "Intellectual Property Rights and North-South Trade." In Ronald W. Jones and Anne O. Krueger, eds., *The Political Economy of International Trade*. Cambridge: Basil Blackwell, pp. 90–107.

Cho, Yoon-Je. 1988. "How the United States Broke into Korea's Insurance Market." *World Development*: 483–96.

Corden, W. Max. 1984. "The Normative Theory of International Trade." In Ronald W. Jones and Peter B. Kenen, eds., *Handbook of International Economics* 1. New York: North Holland, pp. 63–130.

Council of Economic Advisers. 1992. *Economic Report of the President, 1992*. Washington, D.C.: Government Printing Office, 1992.

Council of Economic Advisers. 1994. *Economic Report of the President, 1994*. Washington, D.C.: Government Printing Office.

Crandall, Robert W. 1984. "Import Quotas in the Automobile Industry: The Costs of Protection." *Brookings Review* (Summer).

Dam, Kenneth. 1970. *The GATT: Law and the International Economic Organization*. Chicago: University of Chicago Press.

Dam, Kenneth. 1971. "Implementation of Import Quotas: The Case of Oil." *Journal of Law and Economics* 14: 1–60.

Diebold, William, Jr. 1952. "The End of the ITO." *Princeton Essays in International Finance* 16 (October).

Dunne, Nancy. 1990. "US Sweater Makers Elated by Anti-Dumping Victory." *Financial Times*, September 7, sect. 1, p. 7.

Finger, J. Michael, and Julio Nogues. 1987. "International Control of Subsidies and Countervailing Duties." *World Bank Economic Review* 1: 707–25.

Frank, Charles R., Jr., Kwang Suk Kim, and Larry E. Westphal. 1975. *Foreign Trade Regimes and Economic Development: Korea*. New York: Columbia University Press.

Gardner, Richard. 1956. *Sterling-Dollar Diplomacy*. Oxford: Clarendon Press.

General Accounting Office. 1988. *Evaluation of Market-Oriented Sector Specific Talks.* GAO/NSIAD-88-205. July.

General Agreement on Tariffs and Trade. 1989. *Trade Policy Review: United States 1988.* Geneva: GATT.

General Agreement on Tariffs and Trade. 1992. *Trade Policy Review: United States 1992.* Geneva: GATT.

General Agreement on Tariffs and Trade. 1994. *Trade Policy Review: United States 1994.* Geneva: GATT.

Grossman, Gene M., and Alan B. Krueger. 1991. "Environmental Impacts of a North American Free Trade Agreement." NBER Working Paper No. 3914. Cambridge, Mass.: November.

Haberler, Gottfried. 1933. *Theory of International Trade.* London: William Hodge and Company.

Hudec, Robert E. 1990. "Thinking about the New Section 301: Beyond Good and Evil." In Jagdish N. Bhagwati and Hugh T. Patrick, eds., *Aggressive Unilateralism: America's 301 Trade Policy and the World Trading System.* Ann Arbor: University of Michigan Press, pp. 113–59.

Hufbauer, Gary C., and Kimberly Ann Elliott. 1994. *Measuring the Costs of Protection in the United States.* Washington, D.C.: Institute for International Economics.

Hufbauer, Gary C., and Jeffrey Schott. 1992. *North American Free Trade: Issues and Recommendations.* Washington, D.C.: Institute for International Economics.

Hufbauer, Gary C., and Jeffrey Schott. 1993. *NAFTA: An Assessment.* Washington, D.C.: Institute for International Economics.

Hufbauer, Gary C., Diane T. Berliner, and Kimberly Ann Elliott. 1986. *Trade Protection in the United States: 31 Case Studies.* Washington, D.C.: Institute for International Economics.

Irwin, Douglas. 1994. *Managed Trade: The Case against Import Targets.* Washington, D.C.: AEI Press.

Irwin, Douglas. Forthcoming. "Trade Politics and the Semiconductor Industry." In Anne O. Krueger, ed., *The Political Economy of American Trade Policy.* Chicago: University of Chicago Press for the National Bureau of Economic Research.

Jackson, John H. 1988. "Consistency of Export-Restraint Arrangements with the GATT." *World Economy* 11: 485–500.

Jackson, John H. 1991. *The World Trading System: Law and Policy of International Economic Relations.* Cambridge: MIT Press.

Jackson, John H. 1994. Testimony prepared for the U.S. Senate Finance Committee Hearing on Uruguay Round Legislation. Mimeo. March 23.

Krueger, Anne O. 1990. "The Political Economy of Controls." In Maurice Scott and Deepak Lal, eds., *Public Policy and Economic Development.* Oxford: Oxford University Press, pp. 170–216.

Krueger, Anne O. 1993a. *Economic Policies at Cross Purposes: The United States and the Developing Countries.* Washington, D.C.: Brookings Institution.

Krueger, Anne O. 1993b. "Free Trade Agreements as Protectionist Devices." Paper prepared for Conference on the Occasion of John Chipman's 65th Birthday. University of Minnesota, September 25–26, 1992.

Krueger, Anne O. 1993c. "The Political Economy of U.S. Protection in Theory and in Practice." In Horst Herberg and Ngo Van Long, eds., *Trade, Welfare, and Economic Policies: Essays in Honor of Murray C. Kemp.* Ann Arbor: University of Michigan Press, pp. 215–36.

Krueger, Anne O. Forthcoming. "Political Economy of Trade Protection: Synthesis of Findings." In Anne O. Krueger, ed., *The Political Economy of American Trade Policy.* Chicago: University of Chicago Press for the National Bureau of Economic Research.

Krugman, Paul. 1991a. "Is Bilateralism Bad?" In Elhanan Helpman and Assaf Razin, eds., *International Trade and Trade Policy.* Cambridge: MIT Press.

Krugman, Paul. 1991b. "The Move toward Free Trade Zones." In Federal Reserve Bank of Kansas City, *Policy Implications of Trade and Currency Zones,* proceedings of a symposium held in Jackson Hole, Wyoming, August 22–24, 1991.

Lash, William H., III. 1992a. "Goliath Slays David at the ITC." *Journal of Commerce,* March 17.

Lash, William H., III. 1992b. ". . . In Our Stars: The Failure of U.S. Trade Policy." *North Carolina Journal of International Law and Commercial Regulation* 18 (Fall): 1–56.

Low, Patrick. 1993. *Trading Free: The GATT and US Trade Policy.* New York: Twentieth Century Fund.

McCullogh, Rachel. 1994. "An Asian Capital Crunch? Implications for East Asia of a Global Capital Shortage." In Takatoshi Ito and Anne O. Krueger, eds., *Macroeconomic Linkage: Savings, Exchange Rates, and Capital Flows.* NBER–East Asia Seminar in Economics, vol. 3. Chicago: University of Chicago Press.

Moore, Michael. 1994. "Steel Protection in the 1980s: The Waning Influence of Big Steel?" Paper presented at National Bureau of Economic Research Conference on Political Economy of Trade Protection, February 3–4.

Murray, Tracy. 1991. "Administration of the Antidumping Duty Law." In Richard Boltuck and Robert E. Litan, eds. 1991. *Down in the Dumps: Administration of the Unfair Trade Laws.* Washington, D.C.: Brookings Institution.

Nam, Chong Hyun. 1993. "Protectionist U.S. Trade Policy and Korean Exports." In Takatoshi Ito and Anne O. Krueger, eds., *Trade and Protectionism.* Chicago: University of Chicago Press, pp. 183–218.

Nelson, Douglas. Forthcoming. "Automobiles." In Anne O. Krueger, ed., *The Political Economy of American Trade Policy*. Chicago: University of Chicago Press for the National Bureau of Economic Research.

Nivola, Pietro S. 1993. *Regulating Unfair Trade*. Washington, D.C.: Brookings Institution.

North, Douglass. 1968. "Sources of Productivity Change in Ocean Shipping 1660–1850." *Journal of Political Economy* 76: 953–70.

Orden, David. Forthcoming. "Agricultural Interest Groups and the North American Free Trade Agreement." In Anne O. Krueger, ed., *The Political Economy of American Trade Policy*. Chicago: University of Chicago Press for the National Bureau of Economic Research.

Organization for Economic Cooperation and Development. 1989. *Predatory Pricing*. Paris: OECD.

Park, Yung Chul, and Jung Ho Yoo. 1989. "More Free Trade Areas: A Korean Perspective." In Jeffrey J. Schott, ed., *Free Trade Areas and U.S. Trade Policy*. Washington, D.C.: Institute for International Economics, pp. 141–58.

Passell, Peter. 1994. "Why a Trade Dispute over Roses Is Turning into a Perennial." *New York Times*, August 4, p. C2.

Reich, Robert, and J. Donahue. 1985. *New Deals: The Chrysler Revival and the American System*. New York: Basic Books.

Republic of Korea, Ministry of Trade and Industry. 1989. *Free and Fair Trade: Korea's Record and Commitment*. Seoul.

Richardson, J. David. 1989. "Empirical Research on Trade Liberalization with Imperfect Competition." *OECD Economic Studies* (Spring): 7–50.

Ritchie, Gordon. 1992. "U.S. Protectionism Claims Canadian Casualties." *Wall Street Journal*, March 6, p. A8.

Rugman, Alan M., and Andrew D. M. Anderson. 1987. *Administered Protection in America*. London: Croon Helm.

Scherer, Frederic M. 1992. *International High-Technology Competition*. Cambridge: Harvard University Press.

Schott, Jeffrey. 1989. *Free Trade Areas and U.S. Trade Policy*. Washington, D.C.: Institute for International Economics.

Tsurumi, Yoshi. 1990. "U.S. Japanese Relations: From Brinkmanship to Statesmanship." *World Policy Journal* (Winter 1989–90).

Tyson, Laura d'Andrea. 1992. *Who's Bashing Whom? Trade Conflict in High-Technology Industries*. Washington, D.C.: Institute for International Economics.

U.S. House of Representatives, Committee on Ways and Means. 1991. *Overview and Compilation of U.S. Trade Statutes*. Washington, D.C.: Government Printing Office.

U.S. International Trade Commission. 1988. *Operation of the Trade*

Agreements Program, 1987. 39th Report. Washington, D.C.: Government Printing Office.

U.S. International Trade Commission. 1989. *Operation of the Trade Agreements Program, 1988.* 40th Report. Washington, D.C.: Government Printing Office.

U.S. International Trade Commission. 1990. *Operation of the Trade Agreements Program, 1989.* 41st Report. Washington, D.C.: Government Printing Office.

U.S. International Trade Commission. 1993. *The Year in Trade, 1992.* Washington, D.C.: Government Printing Office.

U.S. Trade Representative. *1992 National Estimate of Trade Barriers.* Washington, D.C.: Government Printing Office, 1992.

Wolf, Martin. 1987. "Differential and More Favorable Treatment of Developing Countries and the International Trading System." *World Bank Economic Review* 2: 647–68.

World Bank. 1993. *World Debt Tables, 1991–1992,* vol. 2. Washington, D.C.: World Bank.

Young, Soogil. 1989. "Trade Policy Problems of the Republic of Korea and the Uruguay Round." Korea Development Institute Working Paper No. 8913.

Index

Access
    by countries to free trade
      agreements, 120
    NAFTA preferential, 97–98
Agricultural policy
    European, 28–29, 120
    Japanese, 28–29
    U.S. import restrictions, 28–30
Agricultural sector
    barriers to imports under GATT,
      28–29
    economic alternatives to
      protection for, 113
    protectionism, 112–13
Anderson, Andrew D. M., 35n, 94
Anderson, Keith B., 41
Antidumping actions
    bilateral nature of laws
      governing, 37
    duties assessment, 47
    under GATT, 35–36
    increase in, 34
    as protection, 48
    protests against U.S., 46
    standards for foreign and U.S.
      firms, 42
    volume and outcome, 37–41
Asia Pacific Economic Cooperation
    (APEC), 99, 121
Association of Southeast Asian
    Nations (ASEAN), 86
Auerbach, Stuart, 89n

Automobile industry
    import restraints for, 56–59, 118
    rules of origin under free trade
      agreements, 95–96

Balance of payments
    effect of protection on current
      account deficit, 17–18
    under GATT provisions, 23
    link of current account deficit to
      fiscal deficit, 116–17
Baldwin, Richard, 14n
Baldwin, Robert E., 2n, 27n, 29n,
    31n, 70n, 71n, 105n
Bangladesh, 48
Beggar-thy-neighbor policies, 21, 26
Beltz, Cynthia, 14n
Berliner, Diane T., 3n, 15n
Bhagwati, Jagdish N., 43, 49n, 106n
Bilateral trade actions
    antidumping, 37
    countervailing duties, 34, 39–41
    defined, 52
    section 301, 64
    Special 301, 68
    Super 301, 36–37, 65
    trade law mandates for, 51
Bilateral trade agreements
    effect of market-opening, 111–12
    incentives of foreign countries to
      use, 53–54
    U.S. policy drift toward, 7–8,
      30–34

VERs and VIEs as, 112, 117–18
See also Multilateral trading
system
Bilateral trade relations
Clinton administration
framework talks, 74, 77
on intellectual property rights,
69
opposition to outcomes, 72
unfair trade practices in, 34
United States with Japan, 72–73
U.S.-Korean, 78–83
U.S. rationale for use of, 78
See also Voluntary export
restraints (VERs); Voluntary
import expansions (VIEs)
Boltuck, Richard D., 34, 41, 43, 49,
119n
Bovard, James, 2, 49n, 76
Brock, William, 87
Bush administration, 59–60, 89

Canada
trade disputes with United
States, 89n
U.S. trade relations with, 53–54,
61
U.S.-Canada Free Trade
Agreement (1988), 88, 94
Caribbean Basin Initiative (CBI), 88n,
90n, 98
Chen, Tain-Jy, 70n, 71n
Chile, 90–91
Chin, Judith, 69
Cho, Yoon-Je, 82
Clinton administration
Chile as member of NAFTA, 98
framework talks, 74, 77
intended expansion of Western
Hemisphere free trade
agreement, 91
MFN status for China, 108
reinstatement of Super 301, 67
setting trade policy, 97
Common Agricultural Policy,
European, 28, 120
Commonwealth preferences, 86
Comparative advantage, 9–11
Corden, W. Max, 85n
Council of Economic Advisers, 24n,
32, 72, 77

Countervailing duties
bilateral nature of laws
governing, 37
under GATT, 36
increase in actions related to, 34
as protection, 48
protests against U.S., 46
volume and outcome, 39–41
Crandall, Robert W., 58
Current account. *See* Balance of
payments
Customs unions, 23, 85n

Dam, Kenneth, 6n, 14n, 22n, 28n, 29,
36n, 85n, 110n
Diebold, William, Jr., 22n
Discrimination
under GATT provisions, 22–23
under Multifiber Arrangement,
62–63
with protection, 12–13, 15
Donahue, J., 57n
Dunne, Nancy, 47
Duties. *See* Antidumping actions;
Countervailing duties

Economic growth
of GATT member countries,
27–28
real world, 7
Economic interests, U.S., 109–10
Elliott, Kimberly Ann, 3n, 15n, 56n,
58n, 60, 63
Employment, 17, 18–19
Enterprise for the Americas, 90
Environmental issues
in NAFTA debate, 91–92
in proposed trade policies, 107
trade policy relation to, 123–24
Uruguay Round negotiations,
103
Escape clause (section 201) actions,
34n, 38, 39–40t
Europe
increased trade, 31–32
U.S. bilateral relations with,
108–9
European Community (EC)
Common Agricultural Policy,
28, 120

economic integration, 86–87
as preferential trading
arrangement, 86–87
European Free Trade Area, 87n
European Payments Union, 26,
86–87
European Union (EU), 72n, 84, 86–87
Export Enhancement Program, U.S.,
112–13

Fair trade principle, 30, 33
Finger, J. Michael, 35n
Fiscal deficit, U.S., 116–17
Foreign policy, U.S.
concerns, 105–9
relation to agricultural and trade
policy, 30
using trade policy at cost to,
107–8
Frank, Charles R., Jr., 79n
Free trade
based on comparative
advantage, 9–11
competition in environment of,
10–11
exceptions to argument for,
13–17
in U.S. national economic
interests, 109–10
U.S. support of principle, 29–30
Free trade agreements
discrimination under GATT
provisions, 23
effect on most-favored-nation
principle, 84
hub-spoke system, 90, 120
proposed U.S.-Mexican, 88–90
proposed Western Hemisphere,
91, 93
rules of origin under, 95–96
U.S.-Canada (1988), 88, 94, 96
U.S.-Israel (1985), 87–88
See also North American Free
Trade Agreement (NAFTA)
(1992)

Gardner, Richard, 20–21n
General Agreement on Tariffs and
Trade (GATT), 5
circumvention, 36–37, 65, 78
dispute resolution mechanism,
22, 27, 33

effect of VIEs and VERs on, 55
fundamental principle, 22–23
intellectual property rights
under, 69
liberalization of trade under, 7
most-favored-nation principle,
84
Multifiber Arrangement under,
62–63
multilateral trade negotiations
under, 26–27
national treatment concept,
24–25
open multilateral trading system
under, 23
preferential trading
arrangements, 85–86
review of U.S. trade practices, 46
rules related to retaliation, 15
secretariat, 25–26
substitution of proposed
Western Hemisphere trade
agreement for, 93–94
Uruguay Round launch, 87
Uruguay Round subsidies
provisions, 24
See also Multilateral trading
system
Generalized System of Preferences,
88n
Goldwater, Barry, 20
Great Depression, 20, 21
Grossman, Gene M., 69n, 92n

Haberler, Gottfried, 6n
Hudec, Robert E., 37, 65n, 66n
Hufbauer, Gary C., 3n, 15n, 56n,
58n, 60, 63, 91n, 95, 98n, 122n

Import restraints. See Voluntary
export restraints (VERs); Voluntary
import expansions (VIEs)
Injury standards
in antidumping cases, 42
disregard of GATT, 63
Trade Act (1974), 38
weakened, 38
Intellectual property rights
under GATT, 69
USTR actions related to, 67–69,
82

rules of origin, 95
sectors excluded from, 91
special interests influencing, 5
U.S. side agreements with
Mexico, 92

Omnibus Trade and Competitiveness
Act (1988)
intellectual property rights
provisions, 68n
Special 301, 67
Super 301, 64–65
Orden, David, 6n

Park, Yung Chul, 80n
Passell, Peter, 35n
Patrick, Hugh T., 43, 49n
Predatory pricing, 42, 118
Protection
arguments against, 11–13
beggar-thy-neighbor, 21
with bilateral trade policy, 8
defense-related argument for, 14
effect on current account deficit,
17–18
effect on domestic production,
12–13
effect on employment levels, 17,
18–19
effect on foreign policy, 110
infant industry argument, 13–14
interest groups seeking, 111–13
national defense as argument
for, 14
national treatment under GATT,
24–25
possible export under NAFTA,
95
relation to U.S. current account
with Japan, 73
response of foreign producers
to, 18
by special interests, 4–5
Protection, administered
antidumping and subsidies
provisions, 37–46
criteria for relief, 111
development in United States,
37–38
effect of, 117
incentives for bilateral
bargaining, 53–54

instrument against individual
country imports, 56
as part of two-sided trade policy,
30–31, 34–35
proposal to alter, 118–19
resentment against U.S., 46
U.S. antidumping orders as, 37,
41
U.S. drift toward, 94
under U.S. trade laws, 34–35
Protection, U.S.
costs of, 63–64
effect of policies, 108
of industries, 15
practices under fair trade
principle, 30, 33

Reciprocal Trade Agreements Act
(1934), 20n
Regionalism, 98
Reich, Robert, 57n
Retaliation with protection, 15
Richardson, J. David, 14n
Ritchie, Gordon, 96
Rugman, Alan M., 35n, 94
Rules of origin, 95

Salinas de Gortari, Carlos, 88–89
Scherer, Frederic M., 13n
Schott, Jeffrey, 89n, 91n, 95, 98n,
122n
Section 201. See Escape clause
(section 201) actions
Section 301
in bilateral bargaining, 64
volume and outcome, 39–40t
See also Super 301
Sectors, economic
exclusion from NAFTA, 91
import restraints in United
States for, 56–64
Market-Oriented, Sector-
Selective (MOSS) talks with
Japan, 73–74
Semiconductor industry
Korean, 118n
relations with Japan, 74–77
U.S.-Japanese agreement (1986),
75–78
SII. See Structural Impediments
Initiative (SII) (1989), U.S.
Smoot-Hawley tariff (1930), 20, 26, 30

137

World Trade Organization (WTO)
    most-favored-nation principle,
      84
    scope and functions of, 102
    U.S. trade policy support for,
      114–15

    under Uruguay Round
      agreement, 22n

Yoo, Jung Ho, 80n
Young, Soogil, 82

About the Author

ANNE O. KRUEGER is professor of economics at Stanford University. She previously taught at Duke University and the University of Minnesota and served as vice president for economics and research at the World Bank. The author or editor of more than thirty books, Ms. Krueger is president-elect of the American Economic Association. She is the recipient of the Frank E. Seidman Distinguished Award in Political Economy, the Kenan Enterprise Award, the Kiel Institute's Bernhard-Harms Prize, and the National Academy of Science's Robertson Prize. Ms. Krueger is a fellow of the American Academy of Arts and Sciences and a member of the Royal Economic Society, the Econometric Society, and the Council on Foreign Relations.

A NOTE ON THE BOOK

This book was edited by
Leigh Tripoli of the AEI Press.
Shirley Kessel prepared the index.
The text was set in Palatino, a typeface designed by
the twentieth-century Swiss designer Hermann Zapf.
Coghill Composition of Richmond, Virginia, set the type,
and Data Reproductions Corporation of Rochester Mills, Michigan,
using permanent acid-free paper, printed and bound the book.

The AEI Press is the publisher for the American Enterprise Institute for Public Policy Research, 1150 17th Street, N.W., Washington, D.C. 20036; *Christopher C. DeMuth*, publisher; *Dana Lane*, director; *Ann Petty*, editor; *Leigh Tripoli*, editor; *Cheryl Weissman*, editor; *Lisa Roman*, editorial assistant (rights and permissions).